Digital Epidemic

Ransoms and hostage data

Fabio Bessega

First edition: March 2025

Disclaimer: The information in this book is provided for informational and educational purposes. The author assumes no liability for any damage resulting from the use of the information contained herein.

To all the people and businesses that have suffered digital attacks, data theft, and privacy breaches: this book is for you.

To the victims who have experienced the frustration, fear and helplessness of seeing their data hostage.

To the professionals who work every day to protect our systems and our information.

And to anyone who believes that, together, we can build a safer digital future.

This book is an invitation not to give up, to learn and to protect yourself.

Preface

In today's digital world, where technology permeates every aspect of our daily lives, the threat of ransomware stands as one of the most insidious and devastating challenges. This book stems from the urgency to understand not only the techniques and operational mechanisms of such attacks, but also the profound psychological, social, economic and legal implications that derive from them.

The foreword of this work aims to prepare the reader for a journey that goes beyond the mere description of ransomware. Criminals operate in an environment of anonymity, where the dehumanization of victims makes their action less morally burdensome. Through true stories and testimonies, we will highlight the destructive power of this form of crime, which does not only affect devices, but threatens people's safety, stability and well-being.

Each chapter is designed to address a unique aspect of ransomware, from its economic consequences to the analysis of existing regulations. We want not only to inform, but also to empower readers, providing them with the tools to defend themselves and face this threat.

In an era where digitalization is constantly expanding, awareness and preparation are the keys to meeting the challenges that lie ahead. It is essential that everyone, from young people to adults, understands the power of cybercrime and how to protect themselves and their information. This book aims to be a guide, an ally in the fight against ransomware, and an invitation to reflect on the ethical and moral choices we face in an increasingly connected world.

I hope that the following pages can inspire you to become not only more informed readers, but also more responsible digital citizens. Security is not just a matter of technology, but a collective commitment to create a safer virtual environment for everyone.

Welcome to this journey of discovery and awareness.

With respect and determination,
Fabio Bessega

Index

Digital Epidemic

Ransoms and hostage data

Chapter 1

Introduction to Ransomware

Imagine waking up one morning to find that all the files on your computer are unreadable. Photos, work documents, important projects: everything is blocked. A message appears on your screen informing you that your data has been encrypted and that you need to pay a ransom to get it back. This is exactly what happens during a ransomware attack.

Ransomware is nothing new. The first example dates back to 1989, when the AIDS Trojan infected thousands of computers via floppy disks, demanding a ransom of $189. Since then, ransomware has become increasingly sophisticated, leveraging advanced technologies such as encryption and cryptocurrencies to make payments anonymous and difficult to trace.

Today, ransomware is one of the most serious cyber threats globally. They affect individuals, companies and institutions, causing enormous economic and social damage. But why are they so widespread? And how can we protect ourselves? In this chapter, we will explore the basics of ransomware, its history, and why it has become such a dangerous threat.

Definition of ransomware

The term ransomware is a combination of two English words: ransom (ransom) and malware (malicious software). As the name suggests, it is a type of malware designed to extort money from victims, blocking access to their files or systems until a ransom is paid.

But how exactly does ransomware work? Imagine opening your computer and discovering that all your files have been encrypted, i.e., turned into an unreadable code. A message appears on your screen informing you that you need to pay a sum of money to regain access to your data, usually in cryptocurrencies such as Bitcoin. This is the essence of a ransomware attack: a digital threat that holds your data hostage until you pay.

The process of a ransomware attack can be divided into three main phases:

Infection: Ransomware enters the victim's system, often through phishing emails, infected file downloads, or software vulnerability exploits.

Encryption: Once inside the system, the ransomware begins encrypting files, rendering them inaccessible. This process is usually quick and quiet, so much so that the victim may not notice anything until it is too late.

Ransom note: After encrypting the files, the ransomware displays a message explaining what happened and how to pay the ransom. The message often includes a countdown timer to increase the pressure on the victim.

Here is an example of a ransom message that you may find on your screen:

> *"Your files have been encrypted! To restore access, you must pay 0.1 Bitcoin (about $8,300). You have 72 hours to make the payment. After this time, your files will be deleted forever."*

This message is designed to scare and convince the victim to pay as quickly as possible. However, paying the ransom does not guarantee that the files will actually be restored, and may even encourage further attacks.

Not all ransomware is created equal. Some simply block access to the system (locker ransomware), while others threaten to publish sensitive data if the ransom is not paid (doxware or leakware). In any case, the goal is always the same: to extort money from victims by exploiting their fear and desperation.

But why is ransomware so effective? The answer lies in their ability to exploit two of our deepest fears: data loss and invasion of privacy. Our files contain memories, personal information, and work data. Losing them means losing a part of ourselves. That's why ransomware is such a powerful and dangerous threat.

To fully understand the threat of ransomware, we need to take a trip back in time, back to the dawn of the digital age. This is where it all began, in a world where computers were still a novelty and the internet was a distant dream for most people.

The origins: The AIDS Trojan (1989)

It was 1989, a time when computers were bulky, floppy disks were state-of-the-art, and the word 'ransomware' didn't yet exist. It was in that year that the world saw the first example of what we would now call ransomware: the AIDS Trojan, also known as PC Cyborg. Created by biologist Joseph Popp, this malware was distributed via floppy disks sent by mail to thousands of users around the world. Once installed, the AIDS Trojan counted the number of times the computer was booted. After 90 boots, it encrypted the names of the files on the machine and displayed a message requesting a payment of $189 to a postal address in Panama.

For many, the AIDS Trojan came as a shock. It was a time when cybersecurity was still a vague concept, and the idea that a computer could be 'infected' was almost inconceivable. Yet, that small floppy disk contained the germ of a threat that would explode decades later.

The evolution: The era of cryptocurrencies (2000s)

Let's move on to the 2000s, a period of rapid technological evolution. The internet was becoming more accessible, and with it came the opportunities for cybercriminals. It was in this decade that ransomware began to become more sophisticated. No longer simple scams based on floppy disks, but real digital extortion tools.

One of the first significant examples was the GpCode ransomware, which emerged in 2004. Unlike the AIDS Trojan, GpCode exploited encryption to make files unreadable, demanding a ransom for the decryption key. However, the real revolution came with the advent of cryptocurrencies, especially Bitcoin. For the first time, criminals could receive payments anonymously and without leaving a trace, making ransomware a lucrative and difficult industry to counter.

Those who remember those years will also remember the feeling of vulnerability that accompanied every new technological discovery. It was a time when computer viruses were still seen as a nuisance rather than a serious threat. But ransomware was about to change everything.

The Modern Era: WannaCry and Beyond (2010–present)

Fast forward to the 2010s, a decade that saw ransomware transform from a sporadic threat to a global phenomenon. The most famous attack of this period is undoubtedly WannaCry, which in May 2017 affected over 200,000 computers in 150 countries, paralyzing hospitals, companies and government institutions. WannaCry exploited a vulnerability in Windows, demonstrating how easy it is for cybercriminals to exploit errors in the systems we use every day.

But WannaCry was just the beginning. In the years since, we've seen increasingly bold and sophisticated attacks, such as NotPetya, which caused billions of dollars in damage, and Colonial Pipeline, which led to fuel shortages in the United States in 2021. These attacks have not only shown the scale of the threat, but have also made it clear that no one is safe: not large companies, not governments, not individuals.

For those who have lived through these years, ransomware has become a symbol of our dependence on technology and our vulnerability to those who know how to exploit it. It is a story that begins with a simple floppy disk and that today involves entire nations, billions of dollars and an uncertain future.

Digital Epidemic

Ransoms and hostage data

Chapter 2

The Technology Behind Ransomware

Ransomware is a phenomenon of extraordinary complexity, a lethal mix of social engineering, software vulnerabilities and cutting-edge encryption techniques. Understanding the technology behind ransomware is not only a critical step in identifying and preventing these attacks, but it is also crucial for developing effective and targeted response strategies. In this chapter, we'll dive into the various technical components that make up ransomware, examining how it actually works, and what vulnerabilities cybercriminals exploit to compromise their victims' systems. Through a detailed analysis, we will try to unravel the mechanisms that make this type of attack so devastating and pervasive in the contemporary digital landscape.

Let's start our journey with a clear and comprehensive definition of ransomware. It is a particular type of malware characterized by the ability to encrypt a computer's files, making them completely inaccessible to the user until a ransom is paid. It is a threat that can manifest itself in different variants, each with its own peculiarities and distinctive methods of attack. This chapter aims to analyze the main categories of ransomware, including:

Cryptographic ransomware: This form is the most common variant, where files are encrypted and the user must pay a sum of money to receive the key necessary for decryption.

Block ransomware: In this mode, the malware not only encrypts files, but also prevents access to the operating system or specific applications, requiring a payment to restore access.

Ransomware as a Service (RaaS): This innovative opportunity in the cybercrime landscape allows criminals to offer malware as a service to other bad actors, receiving a percentage of the ransoms paid. This mode has made ransomware accessible even to those who do not possess high technical skills.

Ransomware can be distributed through a myriad of ways, exploiting vulnerabilities in computer systems or tricking users with cunning. We'll explore the main ways of distribution, including:

Phishing emails: This technique proves to be one of the most common and insidious. Criminals send fraudulent emails containing malicious attachments or links that, when opened, download the malware onto the victim's computer. These emails may appear to be from reputable sources, making it difficult for the user to recognize the scam and prevent infection.

Malvertising: In this scenario, attackers use online advertisements to distribute ransomware. Malicious advertisements can contain malicious code that silently installs on the user's device upon clicking, compromising the system in a sneaky way.

Software vulnerabilities: Another common method is the exploitation of known vulnerabilities in software or operating systems. Criminals can take advantage of outdated or unapplied security patched software to install ransomware. Companies that do not keep their systems up to date are particularly vulnerable to this type of attack.

Once the ransomware has been installed on the victim's system, it begins its attack process, a well-orchestrated and highly efficient mechanism. Let's analyze the inner workings of ransomware, highlighting the key steps in the process:

File encryption: After infection, ransomware starts scanning the system for files to encrypt. It uses strong encryption algorithms, such as AES (Advanced Encryption Standard), to make files unreadable. The speed and efficiency of this process may vary, but in general, ransomware is designed to act quickly and invisibly.

Encryption key generation: During the encryption process, ransomware generates a unique encryption key. This key, which is critical for subsequent file recovery, is often sent to a command-and-control server controlled by attackers, making it even more difficult to recover data without paying the ransom.

Displaying the ransom message: Once the encryption is complete, the ransomware presents the victim with a ransom message. This alert provides detailed instructions on how to proceed with payment, usually in cryptocurrency, and warns of the consequences of non-payment, creating a strong sense of urgency and anxiety in the victim.

Encryption is at the heart of how ransomware works. In this section, we will explore the different encryption algorithms used by criminals and why they are so effective. Attackers tend to choose robust algorithms to ensure that encrypted files are virtually impossible to recover without the decryption key.

We'll also discuss the importance of encryption in data security and how encryption can be used to both protect and compromise information. Businesses need to understand how to implement effective encryption measures to protect their data, thereby reducing the risk of ransomware attacks. We must consider that, if on the one hand encryption is a tool of protection, on the other, in the wrong hands, it becomes a lethal weapon.

Understanding the vulnerabilities that cybercriminals exploit is essential to protecting systems from ransomware threats. We will explore the main vulnerabilities that can be used to compromise systems:

Software and operating system vulnerabilities: Criminals can exploit bugs and vulnerabilities in commonly used software. It is crucial for businesses to keep their systems and applications up-to-date to reduce the risk of attacks. Ignoring updates can prove to be a fatal mistake in cybersecurity.

Misconfigurations: Incorrect system configurations can leave doors open for attackers. It is imperative to follow security best practices to ensure that systems are configured securely. Even small set-up failures can result in serious vulnerabilities.

Social engineering: Many ransomware attacks begin with user manipulation. Cybercriminals can use social engineering techniques to trick people into providing sensitive information or installing malware. Training staff on how to recognize these techniques is crucial to prevent attacks, as people are often the weakest point in the security chain.

There are various technological measures that businesses can implement to protect themselves from ransomware. Best practices for cybersecurity are:

Regular backups: The fundamental rule of protecting your data is to take regular backups. In the event of a ransomware attack, having recent backups can allow you to restore your data without having to pay the ransom. We recommend that you keep copies of your data in separate, secure locations to ensure optimal protection.

Intrusion detection systems: Implementing intrusion detection systems can help identify suspicious activity and prevent attacks before they cause significant damage. These systems can act as the first line of defense, alerting network administrators to abnormal activity.

Staff training: Educating employees about ransomware risks and security best practices is crucial. People are often the most vulnerable point in the security chain, and a well-structured training program can significantly reduce the risk of infection.

In conclusion, ransomware is an ever-evolving threat that exploits technical vulnerabilities and behavioral factors. Understanding the technology behind ransomware is essential for developing effective prevention and response strategies. As cybercriminals continue to refine their techniques, it is critical that organizations remain vigilant and take proactive steps to protect their systems and data, knowing that the battle against ransomware is an ongoing and necessary commitment in today's digital landscape.

Digital Epidemic

Ransoms and hostage data

Chapter 3

The Typical Profile of a Ransomware Hacker

As we continue our exploration of the ransomware phenomenon, it's crucial to understand who the individuals behind these attacks are. Identifying the typical profile of a ransomware hacker not only enriches our understanding of the threat, but also gives us valuable insights into developing more effective defense strategies. In this chapter, we will delve into the motivations, skills, emotions, and behaviors of hackers, painting a complex portrait of these enigmatic figures.

Firstly, it is important to consider the education and training of a ransomware hacker. Many of them come from technical backgrounds, having studied computer science, engineering, or related disciplines. However, not everyone is a college graduate; There is a large community of self-taught people who have learned the art of hacking through online forums, tutorials, and hacker communities. These individuals are often motivated by an insatiable curiosity about how computer systems work, prompting them to test and overcome established barriers. Their technical prowess translates into a deep understanding of software and network vulnerabilities, allowing them to develop and implement sophisticated attacks.

A crucial aspect of a ransomware hacker's profile is their entrepreneurial mindset. Many hackers don't just launch random attacks; on the contrary, they operate as real entrepreneurs in the world of cybercrime. They exploit ransomware as a business model, developing tools and malware that can be sold to other criminals. This commodification of computer skills has led to the emergence of well-organized black markets, where resources, information and services are exchanged. Competition is fierce, and the most skilled and creative hackers earn a reputation and become a benchmark in their field.

From a psychological point of view, ransomware hackers can present complex and conflicting traits. Many of them feel a sense of power and control when they manage to overcome the defenses of a system, feeling an adrenaline rush similar to what an athlete can feel during a competition. However, this thrill can be accompanied by a deep emotional disconnection. Some hackers may justify their actions as a form of protest against a system they perceive as unfair, while others may be driven by a desire for personal revenge or the idea of "punishing" companies they consider immoral. In this way, a narrative is developed that allows them to move away from moral responsibility for the consequences of their actions.

Another significant element is the hacker community. The dark web environment offers spaces for these individuals to meet and collaborate, creating a network of support and sharing. Forums and chat rooms allow hackers to exchange information, tips and strategies, fueling a culture of emulation and competition. Within these communities, the ability to create malware, the ability to carry out attacks, and even the ability to evade law enforcement are elements that confer status and respect. This culture of "doing" and "sharing" not only increases their competence, but also nurtures a sense of belonging and identity.

Furthermore, planning ransomware attacks is a meticulous process. Hackers spend time and resources gathering information about their victims, analyzing weaknesses and vulnerabilities in computer systems. They use social engineering techniques to gain access to sensitive data, impersonating trusted figures or exploiting victims' curiosity. This preparation phase is crucial; The more detailed their understanding of the target, the more likely the attack will be to succeed.

The typical profile of a ransomware hacker is further complicated by their adaptability and resilience. As technologies and countermeasures by companies and government authorities evolve, hackers must continually update their techniques and strategies. The ability to innovate and adapt to new challenges thus becomes a distinctive trait, making them formidable adversaries in the field of cybersecurity.

Finally, it is essential to consider the legal and moral consequences of a ransomware hacker's actions. Many of these individuals are faced with the dilemma of paying the ransom. While they may be motivated by economic necessity, paying a ransom can lead to a cycle of violence and exploitation, fueling further attacks and reinforcing cybercrime. Their position within this cycle of action and reaction can generate inner conflicts, as they have to confront the reality of lives destroyed by their actions.

In conclusion, the typical profile of a ransomware hacker is multidimensional and complex. Understanding their motivations, skills, and psychology is crucial to addressing this growing threat in the digital world. Only through a thorough understanding of these individuals and their dynamics can we hope to develop effective prevention and response strategies, thus protecting potential victims and mitigating the impact of ransomware on society.

Digital Epidemic

Ransoms and hostage data

Chapter 4

Ransomware and Geopolitics

In the digital age, the concept of war has taken on new forms, evolving beyond the traditional battlefield to embrace cyberspace. Among the most insidious and devastating weapons in this new landscape is ransomware, a type of malware that not only compromises information security, but can also serve as a tool of political and strategic aggression. This chapter will explore the role of ransomware in geopolitical conflicts, analyzing how cyberattacks can be used as tools of war, the motivations behind such attacks, and the long-term consequences for international relations.

First, it is crucial to recognize that ransomware has become an extension of existing geopolitical tensions. Nations, particularly those with advanced technological capabilities, have begun to see cyberspace as a new battlefront. Ransomware attacks can be used to destabilize adversaries, damage their economies, and undermine public trust in institutions. This use of ransomware as a cyberweapon is often part of a broader strategy of asymmetric warfare, in which nations seek to gain advantages without direct recourse to conventional military forces.

A prime example of how ransomware can be used in this context is the attack on the computer system of the Hollywood Presbyterian Medical Center hospital in 2016, where hackers demanded a ransom in Bitcoin. While the attack was not directly associated with a specific nation, it demonstrated how critical infrastructure can be vulnerable and how ransomware attacks can have devastating consequences. The global and anonymous nature of ransomware further complicates the geopolitical landscape, making it difficult to attribute responsibility to specific actors and incentivizing the proliferation of such attacks among state-sponsored hacker groups or organized criminals.

Another crucial aspect to consider is the role of nations in supporting or tolerating hacking groups that weaponize ransomware. In some cases, states can use these groups as proxies, allowing them to operate without interference in exchange for support in other areas, such as intelligence gathering or political influence. For example, some reports have suggested that North Korea uses hackers to fund its nuclear program through targeted ransomware attacks. This creates a situation where ransomware becomes not only an attack tool, but also a means of obtaining vital economic resources in a context of international sanctions.

The consequences of such ransomware attacks are not limited to individual events. They can have far-reaching repercussions on a nation's economic and political stability. When critical infrastructure, such as health, energy, or transportation, is hit, the result is often a disaster comparable to that of a traditional military attack. Nations may find themselves having to invest significant resources to restore services and improve cybersecurity, diverting funds from other national priorities. Citizens' loss of trust in institutions can lead to internal instability and a decrease in government legitimacy.

In addition, ransomware has the ability to affect diplomatic relations. Attacks can trigger a cycle of retaliation, in which a nation responds to a cyberattack with equivalent countermeasures or even direct attacks, creating a climate of growing tension. International alliances can be put to the test, as countries seek to respond to common threats and establish a united front against the misuse of technology. However, the lack of clear international norms regarding cyberwarfare makes it difficult to set red lines and manage responses.

Another aspect to consider is the increasing militarization of cyberspace. With the recognition of ransomware's potential as a tool of warfare, many nations are investing in offensive and defensive capabilities in cyberspace. This means that protection against ransomware attacks is not just a matter of cybersecurity, but becomes an integral part of national military strategies. States are developing specialized units to deal with cyber threats, and this can lead to an escalation of tensions, as nations compete to maintain technological superiority.

However, the geopolitics of ransomware is not just a matter of conflicts between states. Non-governmental organizations, companies and activist groups can also get involved. For example, "hacktivist" hacking groups may use ransomware to target companies or governments that they consider immoral or corrupt. In this way, ransomware becomes a means of expressing dissent and trying to influence social or political change. This more complex dimension of ransomware geopolitics underscores how difficult it is to label attackers as "good" or "bad," as motivations can vary widely.

In conclusion, ransomware has taken on an increasingly important role in the modern geopolitical context. Ransomware attacks are no longer just a cybersecurity issue, but have become tools of war, used to gain strategic advantages and influence international relations. The anonymous and global nature of these attacks further complicates the issue, making it difficult to hold accountable and manage retaliation. As the militarization of cyberspace increases and new alliances and rivalries emerge, ransomware will continue to be a crucial element in the geopolitics of the future. Understanding these dynamics is essential to develop effective protective measures and to address the challenges that lie ahead in today's interconnected world.

Digital Epidemic

Ransoms and hostage data

Chapter 5

The Impact of Ransomware on People

In recent years, ransomware has emerged as one of the most serious threats in the cybersecurity landscape. While economic and technical damage is often the focus, it's also crucial to understand the human impact these attacks cause. Ransomware victims are not just numbers or statistics; They are individuals with stories, families and lives that are turned upside down by traumatic experiences. In this chapter, we will examine how ransomware attacks affect people on an emotional, social, and psychological level, as well as the long-term repercussions that can result from such experiences.

When a person becomes the victim of a ransomware attack, the initial reaction is often one of shock and disbelief. The awareness of having lost access to one's data, sometimes vital, can generate a series of emotions, including fear, anxiety and frustration. This chapter will explore how these initial emotions can manifest and influence victims' behavior.

Anxiety is one of the most common responses. Victims may fear that they have lost crucial information such as work documents, personal photographs, or financial data. The fear of not being able to restore this data can lead to a spiral of negative thoughts, in which the victim feels trapped and helpless. This state of agitation can have long-term effects, leading to mental health problems such as chronic anxiety and depression.

The identity crisis is another significant aspect of the emotional impact of ransomware. When people experience an attack, they may begin to question their technological proficiency and their abilities to protect themselves. This can lead to feelings of shame and guilt. "Why didn't I take precautions? How could I have been so naïve?" These questions can haunt victims and contribute to a sense of vulnerability.

In addition, data loss can be seen as a loss of control over one's life. Digital information is increasingly integrated into our identities; Losing access to this information can make people feel like they've lost a part of themselves. This chapter will highlight the personal experiences of some victims, exploring how such attacks affected their self-perception and confidence in their abilities.

The impact of ransomware is not limited to the individual; it also has social consequences. Victims may feel isolated and stigmatized, leading them to avoid social interactions or hide their experience from others. This isolation can be amplified by the fear of being judged or blamed for the attack suffered.

In some communities, the stigma of ransomware victims can be so pronounced that people feel compelled to keep their experience a secret. Lack of social support can compound trauma and make it more difficult for victims to recover. This chapter will discuss how society needs to address this stigma and create a supportive environment for those who have suffered attacks.

In addition to the emotional and social impact, ransomware victims also face significant economic consequences. In many cases, businesses that suffer a ransomware attack may find themselves forced to pay a ransom to regain access to their data. However, even if the ransom is paid, there is no guarantee that the data will be returned or that the system will not be compromised again.

Small and medium-sized enterprises are particularly vulnerable to these economic consequences. They often lack the resources they need to deal with a ransomware attack and recover from it. An attack can lead to immediate financial losses, but also to long-term damage in terms of reputation and customer trust.

As the number of ransomware attacks has increased, it has become increasingly apparent that victims need psychological support. However, they often do not seek help for fear of being judged or the belief that their experiences are not "bad enough" to warrant professional intervention. This chapter will explore the importance of providing psychological support to ransomware victims and the resources available to those seeking help.

Organizations and companies must be proactive in providing assistance to victims. This may include offering counseling services, peer support, and resilience education programs. Awareness of the psychological impact of such attacks is essential to ensure that victims receive the support they need to deal with the consequences of their experiences.

Despite the deep wounds that can result from a ransomware attack, many victims find the strength to recover and rebuild their lives. Through the sharing of their experiences, these people can inspire others to find strength within themselves and not give up in the face of adversity.

Resilience is not just a matter of overcoming trauma, but also of learning from it. Victims can become more aware of the risks, better prepared for future threats, and more motivated to share their experiences with others. This aspect of recovery will be key to fostering a culture of safety and awareness in society.

Digital Epidemic

Ransoms and hostage data

Chapter 6

Ransomware and Economic Consequences

Ransomware isn't just a cybersecurity issue; It is a far-reaching economic issue that affects individuals, companies, and entire industries. Ransomware attacks can have devastating consequences, not only immediately visible, but also long-term. This chapter will explore in detail the economic repercussions of such attacks, analyzing the direct and indirect costs, productivity losses, and challenges victims face in recovering.

When an organization is hit by a ransomware attack, one of the first costs that emerge is that of the ransom itself. In many cases, victims are faced with the choice of paying a ransom to regain access to their data or not paying and risking losing vital information. Ransom demands can vary enormously, from a few hundred to millions of dollars, depending on the severity of the attack and the perceived value of the data.

However, paying the ransom does not always guarantee data recovery. Many victims find themselves paying without getting anything in return, while others find that their systems have been compromised again. This chapter will look at real-world cases of organizations that have faced these decisions, highlighting the ethical and practical dilemma of paying ransoms.

In addition to the direct costs, ransomware attacks also incur significant indirect costs. When an organization is attacked, it can experience disruptions in operations that lead to productivity losses. Employees can find themselves stuck, unable to do their jobs due to a lack of access to essential data. Not only does this affect immediate productivity, but it can also have long-term consequences in terms of reputation and customer trust.

Companies also face the cost of repairing compromised systems. This may include paying cybersecurity experts to investigate the attack, restore data, and implement more robust security measures to prevent future attacks. The costs of these services can add up quickly, creating an additional financial burden for victims.

A ransomware attack can have devastating consequences on an organization's reputation. When a business suffers an attack and customer data is compromised, consumer trust can take a hit. Companies are often forced to deal with increased distrust from customers, who may choose to turn to safer competitors.

Affected businesses can see a decrease in sales and a reduction in customer base, which can have a significant impact on the bottom line. Recovering your reputation takes time and resources, further prolonging the period of economic hardship.

Some industries are more vulnerable to ransomware attacks than others. Healthcare companies, for example, have become frequent targets due to the sensitive nature of the data they handle. An attack on a hospital can not only compromise patient data but also endanger people's lives, as access to systems can be essential for medical care.

After a ransomware attack, organizations face the difficult challenge of recovery. This process includes not only repairing systems and restoring data, but also managing communication with customers and the public. Companies must develop strategies to deal with the crisis, maintain transparency and restore trust.

Digital Epidemic

Ransoms and hostage data

Chapter 7

Ransomware Attacks on Smartphones

In recent years, the use of smartphones has grown exponentially, becoming an extension of our daily lives. These portable devices not only allow us to communicate, but also to manage banking, store personal and professional information, and access a variety of online services. However, as reliance on smartphones has increased, a new frontier in cybersecurity has also emerged: ransomware attacks targeting mobile devices. This chapter will explore how the attack occurs, the consequences for users, and the protective measures that can be taken.

Let's start by examining the nature of ransomware attacks on smartphones. Unlike traditional ransomware attacks that target computers, attacks on mobile devices can happen in various and creative ways. Cybercriminals can exploit vulnerabilities in Android or iOS operating systems, use malicious applications, or send phishing links via SMS or email. Once the user interacts with the malicious content, the ransomware can infiltrate the device, encrypt the data, and demand a ransom for recovery.

A significant example of a ransomware attack on smartphones was the "SLocker" ransomware, which affected Android devices in 2016. SLocker infiltrated devices through apps downloaded from unofficial sources and encrypted the user's files, displaying a message demanding a ransom for recovery. This attack highlighted how vulnerable the Android system is and how important it is for users to pay attention to where the apps they install come from. Similarly, similar attacks have been reported on iOS devices, although iOS tends to be more protected due to its closed ecosystem and Apple's strict guidelines.

One of the main reasons why smartphones have become an attractive target for attackers is the amount of sensitive data stored and access to critical information. Messaging apps, banking applications, and social media are just a few of the sources of data that can be compromised. When a ransomware attack hits a mobile device, the impact can be devastating: users can lose access to their personal files, photos, documents, and even financial information. The fear of losing valuable data can lead many to consider paying the ransom, creating an incentive loop for criminals.

In addition, ransomware attacks on smartphones are particularly insidious because they can happen without the user noticing. Often, malicious apps disguise themselves as legitimate applications, tricking users into downloading them. This leads to a crucial question: how informed are users about the risks associated with using smartphones? Cybersecurity awareness must be a priority, and users must be educated on how to recognize warning signs.

To protect their devices from ransomware attacks, users can take a variety of preventative measures. Firstly, it is crucial to only download apps from official sources, such as the Google Play Store or Apple App Store, where apps undergo security checks. Second, keeping your operating system and installed apps up-to-date is crucial to reduce the risk of vulnerabilities. Updates often contain security patches that address known issues and protect devices from attacks.

Additionally, installing antivirus and security software on mobile devices can offer an extra layer of protection. These tools can detect and block potential threats, reducing the likelihood of infection. Users should also turn on two-factor authentication for sensitive apps, adding an extra layer of security that makes it harder for attackers to access data.

Finally, it is important to educate users on everyday security practices, such as not clicking on suspicious links and not opening messages or emails from unknown senders. Ongoing cybersecurity training can help create a culture of protection among users, making it more difficult for cybercriminals to exploit human vulnerability.

Digital Epidemic
Ransoms and hostage data

Chapter 8

Case Study: Famous Ransomware Attacks

In recent years, the cybersecurity landscape has been disrupted by large-scale ransomware attacks that have highlighted the vulnerability of organizations and the devastating impact of such events. This chapter will explore some of the most well-known cases of ransomware attacks, analyzing how attackers operate, the consequences for victims, and lessons learned that can help prevent future similar incidents.

Locky - The Ransomware That Struck in 2016

Locky was one of the most notorious and destructive ransomware of 2016, marking a significant shift in the cyber threat landscape. Its rapid spread and ingenious use of phishing emails led many victims to a ransom that was difficult to ignore, making it a memorable event in the world of cybersecurity.

Locky was mainly spread through emails containing infected file attachments or links to malicious sites. These emails, often disguised as legitimate communications, were designed to trick victims into opening infectious documents. Once opened, the ransomware encrypted the files on the victim's computer, using unique extensions to denote the encrypted files. The ransom notes ranged from several hundred to thousands of dollars in Bitcoins and were accompanied by detailed instructions on how to make the payment.

The consequences were devastating, with companies and individuals unable to access their data. Locky has affected a wide range of industries, including healthcare, finance, and education, causing operational disruption and significant economic damage. The ease with which ransomware spread highlighted the vulnerability of people and organizations to increasingly sophisticated social engineering techniques.

The Locky attack prompted organizations to review their cybersecurity policies. It became apparent that proper preparation was essential to prevent similar attacks in the future. Companies have begun to invest in advanced security solutions, staff training on phishing detection, and data backup strategies to ensure critical information is protected.

Locky was a clear warning about the need for proper cybersecurity training and training. Its deployment has highlighted how crucial it is to protect systems and data in today's digital world. Fighting ransomware requires a proactive approach and awareness of evolving threats.

Cerber - The Ransomware-as-a-Service of 2016

Cerber made its appearance in 2016, marking a major evolution in the world of ransomware. With its "ransomware-as-a-service" model, Cerber has made cybercrime accessible to a wider audience, increasing the number of attacks and the severity of cyber threats. This ransomware has captured attention for its sophistication and the devastating impact it has had on many organizations.

Cerber spread through phishing emails and exploit kits, infiltrating victims' computers. Once activated, the ransomware encrypted files and generated a ransom message that presented itself in several languages, increasing its chances of affecting a global audience. The ransom note, usually in Bitcoin, was accompanied by detailed instructions on how to make the payment. Cerber's developers also offered a user-friendly interface for victims, making payment easier and more straightforward.

Cerber has had a devastating impact on hundreds of thousands of computers, generating huge profits for its creators. This ransomware has affected a wide range of industries, including healthcare, education, and financial services, causing significant disruption and economic damage. Its popularity has prompted many companies to reconsider their cybersecurity measures and strengthen their defenses against future attacks.

The emergence of Cerber highlighted the importance of proper preparedness in the fight against ransomware. Organizations have begun to invest in advanced security technologies, staff training on how to recognize phishing attempts, and data backup strategies to mitigate the risk of future attacks. It became clear that awareness and training were key to preventing such attacks.

Cerber has shown that the evolution of ransomware not only increases the amount of attacks, but also their complexity and impact. This ransomware has paved the way for a new way of operating in cybercrime, emphasizing the importance of investing in robust and proactive cybersecurity measures. Fighting ransomware requires constant commitment and a willingness to adapt to an ever-changing threat landscape.

WannaCry - The Global Attack of 2017

In May 2017, WannaCry shocked the entire world with a ransomware attack that affected over 200,000 computers in more than 150 countries. By using a vulnerability in the Windows operating system, WannaCry has forever changed the perception of ransomware, demonstrating how devastating a cyberattack can be on a global scale.

WannaCry exploited the EternalBlue vulnerability, a security flaw discovered in Microsoft's software suite. This vulnerability allowed the ransomware to spread on its own through unsecured networks, infecting computers and encrypting files within minutes. Once activated, WannaCry demanded a ransom in Bitcoin, with a countdown timer increasing the pressure on victims to make the payment. The ransom message was threatening and warned that the files would be destroyed if the payment was not made within the stipulated timeframe.

The WannaCry attack caused damage estimated at billions of dollars, affecting hospitals, companies and public institutions. In particular, the British health service (NHS) has been severely affected, with many hospitals forced to close wards and postpone surgical operations. The collective reaction to the crisis has led to increased awareness regarding cybersecurity, emphasizing the importance of keeping systems up-to-date and secure.

The WannaCry outbreak has prompted many organizations to review their cybersecurity policies. It became apparent that it was essential to apply security patches in a timely manner and invest in advanced security solutions. In addition, training staff on how to recognize cyber threats and phishing techniques has taken on a critical role in preventing future attacks.

WannaCry was a clear warning about system vulnerabilities and the potentially catastrophic impact of a ransomware attack on a global scale. Its deployment has highlighted the need for robust cybersecurity and adequate preparedness to deal with emerging threats. The fight against ransomware requires a proactive approach and continuous vigilance to ensure the protection of data and infrastructure in today's digital world.

NotPetya - The Destructive Malware of 2017

In June 2017, NotPetya caused a wave of panic and confusion in the cybersecurity world, initially appearing as a ransomware attack, but actually proving to be highly destructive malware. This attack mainly affected Ukraine, but quickly spread globally, causing enormous damage to large companies and institutions around the world.

NotPetya spread through a vulnerability similar to the one exploited by WannaCry, using the EternalBlue protocol to infiltrate systems. Its mode of attack was deceptive: once activated, NotPetya encrypted victims' files, but unlike traditional ransomware, it was not designed to allow data recovery. This made it a real tool of sabotage rather than a means of extorting money. Victims received a ransom message that looked similar to those of other ransomware, but the malware had no intention of unlocking the files, making the attack highly destructive.

NotPetya caused damage estimated at more than $10 billion, affecting major companies such as Maersk, Merck, and the Ukrainian train service. Operational disruptions have been devastating, with many companies forced to shut down their operations entirely due to loss of access to data. This attack has highlighted how cyber attacks can have consequences far beyond simple ransom, causing incalculable economic and reputational damage.

The spread of NotPetya has prompted many organizations to review their cybersecurity measures. It has become crucial to apply security patches promptly and invest in advanced protection solutions. In addition, companies have begun to implement more robust backup strategies to ensure that data can be restored in the event of an attack. Training staff on how to recognize cyber threats has become a priority, as most attacks begin with human interaction.

NotPetya has shown that cyber attacks can have geopolitical and destructive consequences, revealing the importance of proactive cybersecurity. This attack marked a turning point in the fight against ransomware and highlighted the need for continued preparedness and vigilance. The fight against malware requires an ongoing effort to ensure that critical infrastructure and sensitive data are protected in today's digital landscape.

Ryuk – Targeted Ransomware of 2018

Ryuk emerged in 2018 as one of the most feared and targeted ransomware in the cybercrime landscape. With a highly strategic approach and an ability to adapt to the needs of cybercriminals, Ryuk has proven to be a formidable threat, primarily targeting large companies and institutions.

Ryuk was frequently spread through phishing campaigns and targeted attacks. Attackers often used social engineering techniques to infiltrate systems, tricking victims with seemingly legitimate emails that contained infected attachments or links to malicious sites. Once infiltrated, the ransomware encrypted files encrypted and demanded significant ransoms, ranging from tens of thousands to millions of dollars. The ransom note was typically made in Bitcoin, with detailed instructions on how to proceed with the payment.

The aftermath of the Ryuk attacks has been devastating, with companies across various industries forced to halt their operations due to the loss of access to critical data. Ryuk has targeted hospitals, government bodies and large companies, causing enormous economic and reputational damage. The targeted nature of the attacks, coupled with high ransom demands, has made Ryuk one of the most dangerous and respected ransomware in the cybercrime world.

The rise of Ryuk has led many organizations to reevaluate their cybersecurity measures. It has become crucial to apply security patches promptly, invest in advanced protection solutions, and train staff on how to recognize phishing attempts and other social engineering techniques. In addition, many companies have begun to implement more robust backup strategies to ensure data recovery in the event of an attack.

Ryuk highlighted the growing professionalization of cybercrime, with increasingly sophisticated and targeted attacks. Its ability to adapt and respond to victims' defenses has made it a formidable adversary in the ransomware landscape. The fight against Ryuk and similar threats requires an ongoing commitment to cybersecurity, highlighting the importance of investing in proactive measures to protect data and infrastructure in today's digital world.

GandCrab - The Successful Ransomware of 2018

GranCrab has emerged as one of the most insidious and prolific ransomware in the cybercrime landscape since its debut in 2018. With an aggressive dissemination strategy and a quasi-corporate operational structure, GranCrab indiscriminately targeted companies, institutions and individuals, causing enormous economic damage and a climate of fear among the victims. Its ability to evolve rapidly has made it difficult for cybersecurity authorities and organizations to keep up with its increasingly sophisticated techniques.

GranCrab was primarily spread through phishing campaigns, exploiting malicious emails and infected attachments to infiltrate victims' systems. The attackers used social engineering techniques to convince people to open seemingly harmless files, such as documents or invoices. Once executed, the ransomware would start a process of encrypting files, blocking access to data and leaving victims in a state of distress. The ransom notes, which ranged from a few hundred to several thousand dollars, were communicated through a web interface that provided detailed instructions for paying in Bitcoin. GranCrab not only encrypted the data, but also threatened to publish sensitive information if the ransom was not paid, further increasing the pressure on victims. GranCrab's impact has been devastating, with thousands of businesses and individuals affected around the world. The loss of access to critical data has forced many organizations to temporarily shut down their operations, leading to significant disruptions and financial losses. Sectors such as healthcare, education and public services were among the hardest hit, with hospitals and government institutions forced to resolve emergency situations. The fear of similar attacks has led to an increase in demand for more robust cybersecurity solutions and a greater focus on educating staff about the risks associated with phishing.

The rise of GranCrab has prompted many organizations to review their cybersecurity policies. It has become crucial to invest in advanced security software, implement intrusion detection systems, and train employees on how to identify suspicious emails and social engineering techniques. In addition, creating regular and secure backups has proven to be a crucial strategy for mitigating the impact of a ransomware attack. Cybersecurity authorities also stepped up efforts to monitor and neutralize GranCrab's operations, eventually leading to the disruption of its operations in 2019.

GranCrab has represented a significant evolution in the ransomware landscape, highlighting the increasing professionalization of cybercrime and the need for a proactive approach to cybersecurity. Its ability to adapt to victims' defenses and exploit existing vulnerabilities has made it a formidable adversary. Fighting ransomware like GranCrab requires constant commitment and evolving security strategies, emphasizing the importance of protecting data and infrastructure in the modern digital world.

Maze - Innovative Ransomware of 2019

Maze has emerged as one of the most sophisticated and feared threats in the ransomware landscape as of 2019. With an innovative approach that combines data encryption with the publication of sensitive information, Maze has marked a change in the way cybercrime groups operate, increasing the level of risk for victims. This ransomware has affected a wide range of industries, from technology companies to government institutions, with devastating consequences for data security and the reputation of organizations.

Maze spread through phishing techniques and vulnerabilities in computer systems, often using infected attachments or links to malicious websites to trick users. Once infiltrated, the ransomware not only encrypted files, but also began extracting sensitive data from victims' networks. The attackers, in fact, adopted a two-pronged strategy: encrypting the data and threatening to disclose confidential information if the ransom was not paid. The ransom demands, which ranged from tens of thousands to millions of dollars, were communicated via a dedicated web portal, where victims found detailed instructions for paying in Bitcoin. This tactic has increased pressure on organizations, forcing them to make quick and often burdensome decisions.

The consequences of Maze's attacks have been devastating and far-reaching. Many businesses have experienced significant disruptions to operations, with the loss of access to critical data leading to production shutdowns and massive economic damage. Sectors such as healthcare, education and financial services were among the hardest hit, with hospitals and institutions having to deal with emergency situations. Additionally, the fear of having sensitive data leaked has prompted many organizations to review their security policies and invest in more robust protection measures, making Maze a threat that has left an indelible mark on the cybersecurity industry.

In response to the growing threat of Maze, many organizations have stepped up their cybersecurity measures. It has become critical to implement advanced security solutions, such as intrusion detection systems and anti-malware software, as well as conduct regular security audits to identify vulnerabilities. Staff training has become a priority, with programs that aim to raise awareness of the risks of phishing and best practices for data management. In addition, creating regular backups and keeping them in isolated environments have been adopted as key strategies to ensure data recovery in the event of an attack.

Maze has represented a significant evolution in the ransomware landscape, showing how cybercrime groups are becoming increasingly sophisticated and organized. Its combination of cipher and threat of disclosure has made this ransomware a formidable adversary, requiring a proactive and strategic response from organizations. The fight against Maze and similar cyber threats requires an ongoing commitment to security and a constant evolution of defensive strategies, emphasizing the importance of protecting data and infrastructure in today's increasingly complex digital environment.

Sodinokibi (REvil) - The Ransomware of 2019

Sodinokibi, also known as REvil, has emerged as one of the most dangerous and sophisticated ransomware in the cybercrime landscape since 2019. This ransomware has attracted attention for its highly organized operational structure and how it has exploited vulnerabilities in corporate systems to inflict considerable damage. With a targeted attack strategy that combines data encryption with extortion, Sodinokibi has targeted a wide range of industries, from small and medium-sized companies to large multinational corporations, causing serious economic and reputational consequences.

Sodinokibi spreads through phishing campaigns and vulnerabilities in software, often taking advantage of outdated or poorly configured systems. Attackers use deceptive emails and infected attachments to compromise victims' systems. Once infiltrated, the ransomware initiates an encryption process, blocking access to critical files and creating a crisis situation for the affected organizations. Sodinokibi's distinctive strategy also includes extracting sensitive data, with the threat of publishing it if the ransom is not paid. The ransom demands, which can range from thousands to millions of dollars, are communicated through a dedicated portal, where victims find detailed instructions on paying in cryptocurrency. This dual threat has made Sodinokibi particularly feared in the cybercrime world.

The impact of Sodinokibi's attacks has been devastating, with many companies forced to temporarily shut down their operations due to loss of access to data. Sectors such as health, finance, and utilities were among the hardest hit, suffering significant disruptions and significant economic damage. Organizations have faced not only direct financial losses related to ransoms, but also the costs associated with restoring systems and compromised reputation. The fear that sensitive data could be leaked has prompted many companies to review their security policies, making Sodinokibi a threat that has had a lasting impact on the cybersecurity landscape.

The spread of Sodinokibi has led many organizations to intensify their cybersecurity measures. It has become crucial to apply security patches promptly, invest in advanced security software, and train staff on how to recognize phishing emails and other social engineering techniques. Creating regular backups has been adopted as a key strategy to ensure that data can be recovered in the event of an attack. In addition, cybersecurity authorities have stepped up efforts to monitor and neutralize Sodinokibi's operations, seeking to disrupt cybercriminal networks using it.

Sodinokibi represented a significant step forward in the professionalization of cybercrime, demonstrating how attack groups are becoming increasingly organized and sophisticated. Its ability to combine data encryption and disclosure threats has made this ransomware one of the most formidable adversaries in the cybersecurity landscape. The fight against Sodinokibi requires constant commitment and an evolution of defensive strategies, highlighting the importance of investing in cybersecurity and information protection in today's digital environment.

Egregor - The Ransomware of 2020

Egregor has emerged as one of the most insidious threats in the ransomware landscape as of 2020. With an innovative approach that combines data encryption and theft of sensitive information, Egregor has quickly gained notoriety among cybercrime groups. This ransomware has affected a wide variety of industries, from small and medium-sized companies to large multinational corporations, causing significant economic and reputational damage. Its ability to adapt and exploit vulnerabilities in computer systems has made Egregor a particularly formidable adversary.

Egregor is spread through phishing techniques and vulnerabilities in software, often exploiting deceptive emails and infected attachments to compromise victims' systems. Attackers use social engineering techniques to trick users into opening malicious files, which initiates the process of encrypting data. Once the system was penetrated, Egregor would not only encrypt the files but also begin exfiltrating sensitive data, threatening to publish that information if the ransom was not paid. The ransom notes, which can range from thousands to millions of dollars, were communicated via a dedicated web portal, where victims find detailed instructions for paying in cryptocurrency. This dual threat has greatly increased the pressure on affected organizations.

The impact of the Egregor attacks has been devastating, causing significant disruption to business operations and considerable economic losses. Sectors such as health, education and utilities have been among the hardest hit, with companies forced to temporarily shut down their operations and invest huge resources in restoring systems. Organizations faced direct costs related to paying the ransom, in addition to costs associated with repairing damage and loss of customer trust. The fear of having sensitive data leaked has prompted many companies to revise their security policies, making Egregor a threat that has had a lasting impact in the cybersecurity industry.

In response to the growing threat from Egregor, many organizations have stepped up their cybersecurity measures. It has become crucial to apply security patches promptly, invest in advanced security software, and train staff on how to recognize phishing emails and social engineering techniques. Creating regular backups and keeping them in isolated environments have been adopted as key strategies to ensure data recovery in the event of an attack. Cybersecurity authorities have also stepped up efforts to monitor and neutralize Egregor's operations, working with law enforcement to dismantle the cybercriminal networks behind the ransomware.

Egregor has represented a significant evolution in the ransomware landscape, highlighting how cybercrime groups are becoming increasingly organized and sophisticated. Its combination of data encryption and disclosure threats has made this ransomware a formidable adversary, requiring a proactive and strategic response from organizations. The fight against Egregor and similar threats requires an ongoing commitment to security and a continuous evolution of defensive strategies, emphasizing the importance of protecting data and infrastructure in today's complex digital world.

Clop - The Successful Ransomware of 2020 and Beyond

Clop has emerged as one of the most fearsome and adaptable ransomware in the cybercrime landscape as of 2019. With a strategic and focused approach, Clop quickly gained notoriety for its sophisticated attack techniques and its ability to target large organizations in various industries. This ransomware has proven to be a formidable threat, not only for data encryption, but also for extortion and publication of sensitive information, creating a climate of fear and uncertainty among victims.

Clop spreads through phishing techniques, targeted attacks, and vulnerabilities in computer systems. Attackers use deceptive emails with infected attachments or links to malicious websites to compromise victims' systems. Once infiltrated, Clop begins encrypting critical files, blocking access to data and making it impossible to use it. However, Clop's standout feature is its willingness to exfiltrate sensitive data, threatening to publish it if the ransom is not paid. The ransom notes, which can range from tens of thousands to millions of dollars, are communicated through a dedicated web portal, where victims receive detailed instructions on how to proceed with the cryptocurrency payment. This dual threat makes Clop particularly dangerous, as victims are faced with not only data encryption, but also the risk of leaking confidential information.

The impact of Clop's attacks has been devastating, with many companies forced to halt their operations due to the loss of access to critical data. Sectors such as health, education, finance, and information technology were among the hardest hit, suffering significant disruptions and significant economic damage. Organizations have faced not only the direct financial losses associated with paying the ransom, but also the costs associated with restoring systems and managing compromised reputations. The fear of having sensitive data leaked has further increased the pressure on victims, forcing them to review their cybersecurity policies.

In response to the growing threat of Clop, many organizations have stepped up their cybersecurity measures. It has become crucial to apply security patches promptly, invest in advanced antivirus solutions, and train staff on how to recognize suspicious emails and social engineering techniques. Creating regular backups and storing them in isolated environments have been identified as key measures to ensure data recovery in the event of an attack. In addition, cybersecurity authorities have been working with law enforcement to monitor and neutralize Clop's operations, seeking to disrupt cybercriminal networks using this ransomware.

Clop represented a significant evolution in the ransomware landscape, highlighting how cybercrime groups are becoming increasingly organized and sophisticated in their operations. Its combination of data encryption and disclosure threats has made this ransomware one of the most feared in the cybersecurity industry. The fight against Clop and similar cyber threats requires a constant commitment to security and a continuous evolution of defensive strategies, emphasizing the importance of protecting data and infrastructure in an increasingly complex and vulnerable digital world.

Conti - A High-Profile Ransomware in 2020 and Beyond

Conti has emerged as one of the most devastating and insidious ransomware in the cybercrime landscape as of 2020. With a highly organized approach and targeted attack methodology, Conti has targeted numerous companies in various industries, inflicting significant economic and reputational damage. Its ability to adapt to and exploit vulnerabilities in computer systems has made Conti a formidable threat, attracting the attention of cybersecurity authorities and organizations around the world.

Conti spreads through phishing techniques, vulnerability exploits, and targeted attacks, with a focus on compromising corporate networks. Attackers often use deceptive emails containing malicious attachments or links to malicious websites, managing to penetrate victims' systems. Once access is gained, Conti performs a process of encrypting files, making critical data inaccessible and blocking business operations. Unlike many other ransomware, Conti does more than just encrypt information; It also performs exfiltration of sensitive data, threatening to publish it if the ransom is not paid. The ransom demands can range from tens of thousands to millions of dollars, and are communicated via a secure web portal, where victims can find detailed instructions for paying in cryptocurrency.

The impact of Conti's attacks has been devastating, with many organizations forced to shut down their operations due to the loss of access to data. Critical sectors such as health, finance, education and public infrastructure were among the hardest hit, suffering significant disruptions and significant economic damage. Companies faced not only direct losses related to the ransom, but also the costs associated with restoring systems, managing the crisis, and losing customer confidence. The threat of having sensitive data leaked has further increased the pressure on victims, forcing them to review their cybersecurity policies and implement more robust protection measures.

In response to the growing threat from Conti, many organizations have stepped up their cybersecurity measures. It has become crucial to apply security patches promptly, invest in advanced antivirus solutions, and train staff on how to recognize phishing emails and social engineering techniques. Creating regular backups and storing them in isolated environments have been identified as key measures to ensure data recovery in the event of an attack. In addition, cybersecurity authorities have been working with law enforcement to monitor and neutralize Conti's operations, seeking to disrupt the networks of cybercriminals responsible for this ransomware.

Conti represented a significant evolution in the ransomware landscape, highlighting how cybercrime groups are becoming increasingly organized and sophisticated in their operations. Its combination of data encryption and disclosure threats has made this ransomware one of the most dangerous in the cybersecurity industry. The fight against Conti and similar threats requires an ongoing commitment to security and a continuous evolution of defensive strategies, emphasizing the importance of protecting data and infrastructure in today's complex and vulnerable digital world.

Hive - The Emerging Ransomware in 2021 and Beyond

Hive has emerged as one of the most feared and adaptable ransomware in the cybercrime landscape since its debut in 2021. With a strategic approach and a highly organized operational structure, Hive quickly gained notoriety for its ability to target a wide range of industries, inflicting significant economic and reputational damage. Its combination of data encryption and disclosure threats has made Hive a formidable adversary in the cybercrime world, attracting the attention of cybersecurity authorities and organizations around the world.

Hive spreads through phishing techniques, software vulnerabilities, and targeted attacks. Attackers use deceptive emails, often containing malicious attachments or links to compromised websites, to infiltrate victims' systems. Once access is granted, Hive begins a process of encrypting files, blocking access to critical data and forcing organizations to face an immediate crisis. Unlike many other ransomware, Hive adopts a double-fronted attack strategy: not only does it encrypt data, but it also extracts sensitive information, threatening to publish it if the ransom is not paid. The ransom notes, which can range from thousands to millions of dollars, are communicated through a dedicated web portal, where victims can find detailed instructions on how to proceed with the cryptocurrency payment. This dual threat has made Hive particularly dangerous, as victims are faced with not only data encryption, but also the risk of leaking confidential information.

The impact of Hive's attacks has been devastating, with many businesses forced to halt their operations due to loss of access to data. Sectors such as health, technology, finance, and utilities were among the hardest hit, suffering significant disruptions and significant economic damage. Organizations have faced not only direct losses related to paying the ransom, but also the costs associated with repairing damage and managing the crisis. The fear of having sensitive data leaked has further increased the pressure on victims, forcing them to review their security policies and invest in more robust protection measures.

In response to the growing threat of Hive, many organizations have stepped up their cybersecurity measures. It has become crucial to apply security patches promptly, invest in advanced antivirus solutions, and train staff on how to recognize suspicious emails and social engineering techniques. Creating regular backups and storing them in isolated environments have been identified as key measures to ensure data recovery in the event of an attack. In addition, cybersecurity authorities have been working with law enforcement to monitor and neutralize Hive's operations, seeking to dismantle the cybercriminal networks behind this ransomware.

Hive has represented a significant evolution in the ransomware landscape, demonstrating how cybercrime groups are becoming increasingly organized and innovative in their operations. Its combination of data encryption and disclosure threats has made this ransomware one of the most dangerous in the cybersecurity industry. Combating Hive and similar cyber threats requires an ongoing commitment to security and a continuous evolution of defensive strategies, emphasizing the importance of protecting data and infrastructure in today's complex and vulnerable digital world.

Medusa - The Emerging Ransomware

Medusa is an emerging ransomware that made its appearance in the cybercrime landscape in 2021. This malware has attracted attention for its innovative attack strategy and sophisticated techniques used to infiltrate victims' systems. Known for its aggressiveness and its ability to adapt to different environments, Medusa has quickly established itself as a serious threat to businesses and organizations of various kinds.

Medusa is mainly spread through phishing campaigns and targeted attacks. Attackers use deceptive emails, which often appear to come from trusted sources, to trick victims into clicking on dangerous links or opening infected attachments. Once the malware manages to infiltrate the system, it begins encrypting files, making them inaccessible to victims.

One of Medusa's standout features is its double extortion approach. In addition to encrypting files, attackers also steal sensitive data and threaten to publish it online if the ransom is not paid. Not only does this increase the pressure on victims to pay, but it also creates an additional layer of risk to the reputation of the affected companies.

The consequences of Medusa's attacks can be devastating. Businesses can experience major operational disruptions due to loss of access to critical data. In addition, the threat of sensitive data exposure can compromise the trust of customers and business partners, with long-term repercussions on the organization's relationships and financial strength. Medusa's attacks have affected various industries, highlighting the vulnerability of critical infrastructure and the need for greater protection.

To address the threat of Medusa ransomware, organizations must take a proactive approach to cybersecurity. This includes investing in advanced security technologies, training staff on how to recognize phishing attempts, and implementing data backup strategies. It is critical for companies to develop an incident response plan that includes crisis management and communication with stakeholders.

Medusa is a clear example of the ongoing evolution of the ransomware landscape. Its ability to adapt and use advanced extortion techniques highlights the importance of investing in cybersecurity measures to protect data and infrastructure. Constant vigilance and preparedness are essential to deal with emerging threats like Medusa and ensure the security of organizations in today's digital world.

BlackCat - The Emerging Ransomware

BlackCat, also known as Alphv, is an emerging ransomware that made its appearance in the cybercrime landscape in 2021. This malware has attracted attention for its sophistication, being one of the first ransomware written in Rust, a programming language known for its efficiency and security. With an innovative approach and ransomware-as-a-service model, BlackCat has quickly established itself as a serious threat to businesses and organizations.

BlackCat spreads through phishing techniques and vulnerabilities in systems, infiltrating corporate networks. Once activated, this ransomware encrypted files and demanded a ransom in cryptocurrencies, increasing the difficulty for victims to trace payments. One of the standout features of BlackCat is its double-extortion approach: in addition to encrypting data, attackers steal sensitive information and threaten to publish it online if the ransom is not paid. This creates significant pressure on victims, prompting them to consider paying as a necessary option to protect their data and reputation.

The consequences of BlackCat attacks can be devastating. Affected businesses can experience severe operational disruptions due to loss of access to critical data. Additionally, the threat of sensitive data exposure can compromise the trust of customers and business partners, leading to significant reputational damage. BlackCat's attacks have affected various industries, highlighting the vulnerability of critical infrastructure and the need for greater protection.

To address the threat of BlackCat ransomware, organizations must take a proactive approach to cybersecurity. This includes investing in advanced security technologies, training staff on how to recognize phishing attempts, and implementing data backup strategies. It is critical for companies to develop an incident response plan that includes crisis management and communication with stakeholders.

BlackCat is a clear example of the ongoing evolution of the ransomware landscape. Its ability to adapt and use advanced extortion techniques highlights the importance of investing in cybersecurity measures to protect data and infrastructure. Constant vigilance and preparedness are essential to deal with emerging threats like BlackCat and ensure the security of organizations in today's digital world.

Digital Epidemic

Ransoms and hostage data

Chapter 9

Ethical Dilemmas in Ransom Payment

The first thing to consider is that paying ransoms can fuel a cycle of crime and fear. Every time a victim decides to pay, they send a clear message to the criminals: "There is a profit in this crime." This behavior can encourage further attacks, not only against the company that paid, but also against other entities. Cybercriminals may interpret the payment as a signal of vulnerability, increasing their determination to strike again. Therefore, the legitimization of crime becomes a tangible risk that propagates over time, creating an increasingly dangerous environment.

The legitimization of crime also has significant social impacts. The increasing prevalence of ransomware attacks has led to a climate of anxiety and distrust among businesses and consumers. If victims start considering paying ransoms as a normal solution, this could lead to a normalization of the cybercrime itself. Citizens may feel less safe sharing personal information and doing business online, damaging trust in digital technologies. Society risks finding itself in a vicious cycle in which fear and insecurity become the norm.

The issue of legitimizing crime is further complicated by the lack of a clear regulatory framework. In many countries, there are no specific laws prohibiting the payment of ransoms, leaving victims in a kind of legal limbo. This regulatory vacuum can lead businesses to make hasty decisions, often influenced by the immediate pressure to retrieve vital data. The lack of clear guidelines can contribute to a culture of "easy pay," where crime is seen as a viable option rather than an act to be condemned.

Faced with these dilemmas, it is crucial to explore alternatives to paying the ransom. Cybersecurity experts suggest that companies should invest in proactive security measures, such as regular backups and staff training on cyber risks. In addition, it is important for victims to report attacks to the appropriate authorities, which can help create a database of attacks and improve defense measures. Choosing not to pay the ransom can be a way to fight the legitimization of crime, showing that society will not tolerate such acts.

Paying ransoms in the event of ransomware attacks presents a significant ethical dilemma, with legitimizing crime as one of the most concerning issues. The consequences of these decisions extend far beyond the affected individual and company, affecting society as a whole. It is imperative that businesses and individuals think carefully about their choices and consider alternatives to paying ransoms, thus contributing to a safer and more resilient digital environment. Only by addressing these issues proactively can we hope to break the cycle of crime and fear that ransomware has created.

Employees are one of a company's most valuable assets, and their trust in management is critical to morale and productivity. When a ransomware attack strikes, management must address the question of trust: "How can we assure our employees that we are doing everything we can to protect their data and job positions?" If the company decides to pay the ransom, employees may feel reassured that the organization is trying to resolve the issue. However, there is also a risk that this decision will be perceived as a sign of weakness or lack of preparation, further damaging trust.

Another critical responsibility is the protection of sensitive data, both of employees and customers. Companies have an obligation to implement appropriate security measures to protect personal and business information. If an organization decides to pay a ransom, it may not only not guarantee data recovery but also further expose information to future risks. This begs the question, "Are we really protecting our employees and customers if we choose to pay?" The decision to pay the ransom might appear to be a short-term solution, but it can have long-term consequences for the company's security and reputation.

Companies must also consider the economic implications of paying a ransom. In many situations, the cost of the ransom is only a fraction of the total expenses associated with a ransomware attack. Companies can face significant costs related to lost productivity, the need to restore systems, and legal fees. Additionally, if the company pays a ransom, it could be seen as an easy target for future attacks, resulting in even greater economic losses. Economic responsibility then becomes a dilemma: "Is it wise to invest in a payment that may not guarantee a lasting solution?"

In addition to employees, companies have a responsibility to consider the interests of all stakeholders, including customers, suppliers, and investors. The decision to pay a ransom can affect the company's reputation and its trust in the market. Stakeholders may be wondering, "If the company can't protect data, how can it ensure the quality of its products or services?" This leads to a significant dilemma: companies must balance immediate needs with the long-term impact on stakeholder relationships.

Paying ransoms in the case of ransomware raises important considerations about companies' responsibility to their employees and stakeholders. Decisions made at these critical times can have significant repercussions on the organization's trust, security, and reputation. It is crucial for companies to take a strategic and proactive approach to managing cybersecurity, investing in preventative measures and developing appropriate response plans. Only through responsible and transparent management can companies address the challenges posed by ransomware attacks and maintain the trust of their employees and stakeholders.

Article: The Value of Human Life in the Context of Ransom Payment

In extreme scenarios, such as attacks on healthcare facilities, paying a ransom could be seen as a necessity to save lives. Hospitals, for example, can be targets of ransomware attacks that block access to vital data for patient treatment. In such situations, hospital managers are faced with a moral question: "Is it fair to pay to ensure patient safety?" The value of human life becomes the measure by which the decision to pay the ransom is evaluated.

Paying ransom in situations where human life is threatened raises significant ethical questions. While many might argue that life should be top priority, others might argue that paying the ransom legitimizes criminal behavior and encourages further attacks. The central question becomes: "Is it ethical to feed a crime market in the name of saving lives?" This dichotomy highlights the complexity of the situation, where choices are fraught with moral consequences.

On the other hand, the decision not to pay the ransom can pose equally serious risks. In scenarios where payment could save lives, choosing not to act could lead to devastating consequences. This leads to a deep reflection on a company's duty to its patients or customers. "What is an organization's responsibility to human life?" Organizations must assess the potential impacts of their decisions, balancing ethical considerations with immediate needs.

To address this dilemma, it is essential for organizations to adopt a values-based approach. This implies a deep reflection on what is truly important to the institution, its employees and the community. Companies should develop clear policies regarding their responses to ransomware attacks, integrating ethical considerations into their decision-making. This approach not only helps clarify priorities in crisis situations, but also helps build a company culture that places an intrinsic value on human life.

In ransomware attack scenarios, communication and transparency become critical. Organizations need to be open about their decisions and the reasons behind them. Not only does this help maintain trust between employees and stakeholders, but it also allows you to engage with the community and relevant authorities. Transparency in choices can contribute to a broader debate on policies related to ransomware and the protection of human lives.

The value of human life is a crucial factor to consider in the debate over paying ransoms in the event of ransomware attacks. Companies face complex ethical dilemmas, balancing responsibility for human life with the implications of legitimizing crime. Taking a values-based approach, promoting communication and transparency, and reflecting on one's own decisions are key steps in addressing these challenges. Only in this way can we hope to protect not only the data, but also the lives of the people involved.

One of the main obstacles that companies face in managing ransomware attacks is the lack of a clear regulatory framework regarding the payment of ransoms. In many countries, there are no specific laws that prohibit or regulate such payments. This ambiguity can lead companies to make hasty decisions based on fear rather than an informed strategy. The lack of clear laws means that victims may find themselves having to decide for themselves, creating uncertainty and potential legal consequences.

Law enforcement agencies play a critical role in the fight against cybercrime. However, their ability to intervene in good time and provide support to victims is often limited. Authorities must not only investigate attacks but also educate companies on how to prevent such incidents. Communication between law enforcement and businesses is essential to develop effective response and recovery strategies. However, in many cases, victims may feel reluctant to report an attack, fearing negative repercussions on their reputation.

Government institutions have a responsibility to create an environment that fosters cybersecurity and protects victims of ransomware attacks. This includes developing laws and regulations that set clear guidelines regarding the payment of ransoms. In addition, institutions should provide educational resources and tools to help companies prepare for and respond to such threats. Collectively, institutions can collaborate with the private sector to create security protocols and respond effectively to attacks.

Another key aspect is the promotion of collaboration between the public and private sectors. Institutions should encourage companies to share information about threats and attacks suffered, creating a support network to improve collective resilience. Implementing security information-sharing platforms can help turn the response to ransomware attacks into a community effort, rather than an isolated battle.

Finally, institutions must emphasize the importance of prevention. Investing in cybersecurity awareness and training campaigns can help businesses better understand the risks and take proactive measures. Creating a regulatory framework that incentivizes security and preparedness can reduce the likelihood of ransomware attacks, thereby decreasing the number of situations in which companies have to decide whether or not to pay a ransom.

The role of institutions in the context of paying ransomware ransoms is crucial to address an ever-evolving threat. The lack of clear regulations, the accountability of law enforcement, and the need to promote collaboration between the public and private sectors are all factors that influence victims' decisions. It is essential for institutions to play an active role in creating a safe and resilient environment by providing resources, support and clear regulations. Only through a collective effort can we hope to effectively address the threat of ransomware and protect businesses and consumers from future attacks.

Transparency is essential in any crisis situation. In the event of a ransomware attack, companies have a responsibility to inform their employees, customers, and stakeholders about the situation. Not only does this help maintain trust, but it also allows you to involve people in the response to the attack. Clear and open communication can reduce anxiety and uncertainty, making employees and stakeholders feel part of the solution rather than just spectators of a negative event.

Internal communication is especially crucial in attack situations. Employees should be informed about the nature of the attack, the steps the company is taking to deal with it, and any actions they need to take. Lack of information can lead to confusion and fear, hurting morale and productivity. Companies should establish clear and timely communication channels to keep employees updated and engaged in the recovery process.

External communication, aimed at customers and stakeholders, is equally important. Companies need to address the issue of reputation and trust. In the event of an attack, it is crucial to communicate transparently about the situation, the measures taken to mitigate the damage, and future actions. Not only does this help maintain customer trust, but it also shows that the company is accountable and ready to deal with the consequences of the attack.

When a company decides to pay a ransom, the issue of transparency becomes even more complex. While paying may seem like an immediate solution to recover vital data, the lack of transparency about this decision can damage the company's reputation. Stakeholders may wonder why the company chose to pay and whether this implies a lack of preparation or expertise. Communication regarding the ransom payment should be handled with care, revealing the reasons and context behind this decision.

In addition to communication, companies should document every step of the process, from the initial attack to response and resolution. This documentation not only helps to evaluate the effectiveness of the measures taken, but can also serve as a basis for future security improvements. Transparency in recording actions taken can provide stakeholders with a clear and comprehensive view of incident management, further strengthening trust.

Finally, it is essential for companies to build a culture of transparency not only during crises, but also as a daily operating norm. Organizations should encourage open communication and feedback, creating an environment where employees feel safe reporting potential safety issues and discussing their concerns. A culture of transparency fosters preparedness and resilience, enabling businesses to better address future threats.

Transparency and communication play a crucial role in the context of paying ransoms in the event of ransomware attacks. Companies must be ready to communicate openly with their employees, customers and stakeholders, not only about the current situation, but also about the decisions made. Transparency builds trust, reduces anxiety, and contributes to effective incident management. In an era where cybersecurity is critical, businesses must recognize the importance of communication as an integral part of their ransomware attack response strategies.

Digital Epidemic
Ransoms and hostage data

Chapter 10

Legal and Regulatory Implications on

Cybersecurity

The growing prevalence of ransomware has highlighted the need for a robust and well-defined regulatory framework for cybersecurity. In this context, the applicable regulations are a crucial element for companies, public bodies and individual citizens.

A key aspect to consider is the General Data Protection Regulation (GDPR), which came into force in May 2018. The GDPR introduced stringent requirements for the protection of personal data and required organizations to implement appropriate security measures to prevent breaches. In the event of a ransomware attack, companies are obliged to notify the relevant authorities within 72 hours of discovering the breach, if the personal data of European citizens is affected. This notification requirement is crucial, as it aims to ensure transparency and protection of individuals' rights, but it also poses significant risks for companies, as penalties for non-compliance can be as high as 4% of global annual turnover.

In addition to the GDPR, many jurisdictions have adopted specific laws on breach notification. For example, in the United States, most states have legislation that requires companies to notify customers and regulators in the event of a data breach. The variety of state-level laws can make compliance complex for companies operating in multiple states, forcing them to develop cybersecurity strategies and notification protocols that are appropriate for different regulations.

Another crucial point concerns the legal liability of companies. When a ransomware attack hits an organization, the responsibility can fall on management, employees, or the company itself. Companies must demonstrate that they have taken adequate security measures and complied with applicable regulations to protect data. Negligence in implementing such measures can lead to lawsuits and damages, creating an additional incentive for companies to invest in cybersecurity.

In a context where businesses are often faced with the difficult decision of whether or not to pay the ransom demanded by cybercriminals, it is important to consider ransom payment laws. Some countries, such as the United States, have introduced regulations that penalize the payment of ransoms to terrorist groups, making it difficult for affected companies to decide. Companies must be aware of the legal implications of such a payment and the possible consequences on their legal and reputational status.

Additionally, it is interesting to note how cybersecurity regulations are evolving in response to the rise of ransomware attacks. Lawmakers are working to update existing laws and introduce new measures that address emerging threats. This includes adopting stricter data protection guidelines and incentivizing proactive security practices, such as implementing regular security audits and continuing employee training.

An often overlooked aspect is the role of regulatory authorities. Bodies such as the Italian Data Protection Authority and the Federal Trade Commission in the United States are tasked with monitoring companies' compliance with cybersecurity regulations. These authorities not only apply penalties for violations, but also provide guidelines and support for companies to improve their security practices.

Finally, international collaboration is proving to be increasingly essential in the fight against ransomware. International organizations, such as Interpol and Europol, are promoting initiatives to improve cooperation between countries in sharing information and fighting cybercrime. This collaboration is critical to addressing global threats and developing more effective regulations.

The adoption of the General Data Protection Regulation (GDPR) in Europe has been a significant step in regulating data protection and cybersecurity, but the rest of the world is addressing the issue of data protection and cybersecurity in different ways, depending on jurisdictions and specific local needs. This article will explore some of the most relevant regulations outside of Europe, highlighting the differences and similarities with the GDPR.

In the United States, there is no single federal data protection law equivalent to the GDPR. Instead, the country is characterized by a set of state and federal laws that cover specific industries and types of data. A significant example is the California Consumer Privacy Act (CCPA), which gives California citizens specific rights regarding their personal data, including the right to know, the right to have their data deleted, and the right not to be discriminated against for exercising privacy rights. While the CCPA is not as comprehensive as the GDPR, it represents an important step toward greater data protection in the U.S. and has already inspired other state-level legislation.

In Canada, the Personal Information Protection and Electronic Documents Act (PIPEDA) regulates the collection, use, and disclosure of personal information by organizations in the private sector. PIPEDA requires companies to obtain consent from individuals before collecting their data and grants them the right to access and correct inaccurate information. While PIPEDA shares some similarities with the GDPR, it also has significant differences, such as the absence of such high penalties for violations.

In Australia, the Privacy Act 1988 sets out data protection principles that govern the collection, use and disclosure of personal information. Recently, the Notifiable Data Breaches (NDB) scheme was introduced, requiring organizations to notify data breaches that may pose a serious risk to individuals. This scheme is similar to the notification requirement under the GDPR, but the penalties for non-compliance are lower than in Europe.

In Japan, the Act on the Protection of Personal Information (APPI) is the primary legislation governing data protection. Even though the APPI has undergone significant updates to align more closely with international standards, including those of the GDPR, there are still differences in individuals' rights and compliance practices.

In Brazil, the Lei Geral de Proteção de Dados (LGPD) was implemented in 2020 and is heavily inspired by the GDPR. It establishes similar rights for individuals and imposes obligations on companies regarding the protection of personal data. However, its enforcement and the effectiveness of sanctions are still being developed.

Another significant example is South Korea's Personal Data Protection Law, which has one of the strictest data protection regimes globally. This law requires users' consent for the collection and use of personal data and provides for severe penalties for violations.

In summary, while the GDPR has set an important benchmark for data protection globally, many other jurisdictions are developing their own regulations in response to cybersecurity and data protection challenges. These laws vary greatly in scope, obligations, and penalties, creating a complex landscape for businesses to navigate. In a global context, understanding these regulations is essential to ensure compliance and protect user data, especially in an era when ransomware attacks are on the rise. The growing interconnectedness between nations requires a collaborative and harmonized approach to address cybersecurity threats and ensure the protection of personal data worldwide.

In conclusion, the legal and regulatory implications of cybersecurity in relation to ransomware are complex and constantly evolving. Businesses must navigate a diverse and rapidly changing regulatory landscape, taking proactive steps to ensure data protection and compliance with applicable laws. The growing awareness of the legal implications of ransomware attacks underscores the importance of a well-defined cybersecurity strategy that not only protects data, but also protects the reputation and sustainability of organizations in the long term.

A crucial element in this context is the notification obligation, which sets out the rules for informing the competent authorities and affected individuals in the event of a data breach.

An important aspect to consider is that the notification obligation is not only limited to the competent authorities and affected individuals, but can also extend to third parties and business partners, depending on the nature of the violation. For example, companies may be required to inform their suppliers, customers, and other stakeholders if compromised data could affect their security.

The notification obligation is a key element in the fight against ransomware attacks and in the protection of personal data. Existing regulations, such as GDPR in Europe and state laws in the United States, place a responsibility on companies to act promptly in the event of violations. The increasing interconnectedness between nations and the adoption of similar laws globally suggest that the importance of these obligations will continue to grow.

With regard to the responsibilities of Companies, we can say that it is essential to understand that companies have an obligation to adopt appropriate security measures to protect the personal data of their customers, employees and other interested parties. This obligation is not only ethical, but it is also enshrined in laws such as the GDPR in Europe and the CCPA in California, which stipulate that organizations must implement appropriate technical and organizational measures to ensure a level of data security commensurate with the risks. This includes, for example, the adoption of encryption systems, firewalls, multi-factor authentication and secure access protocols.

When a ransomware attack occurs, the company's liability can vary depending on the circumstances and the preventive measures already taken. If an organization can demonstrate that it has taken all necessary precautions to protect data, it may be less likely to be held liable in the event of a breach. However, if the company has been negligent, such as by failing to update security software or by failing to properly train employees on cyber threat management, it could face serious legal consequences. Penalties for violating data protection regulations can include substantial fines, reputational damage, and legal action by customers or business partners.

Another crucial aspect of corporate liability is the obligation to notify in the event of a data breach. As already discussed, many regulations require companies to inform the relevant authorities and those involved within a specific deadline. Failure to comply with this obligation not only exposes the company to penalties, but can also further undermine customer trust and damage the company's reputation. Organizations must therefore develop incident response plans that include clear procedures for reporting breaches and communicating with stakeholders.

In addition, the responsibility of companies extends beyond the protection of internal data. Organizations that handle third-party data, such as vendors or business partners, must ensure that this data is also protected from ransomware attacks. This implies the need to enter into clear contracts that set out responsibilities in the event of a data breach. Companies must also conduct security audits and assessments on their suppliers to ensure that protective measures are adequate and compliant with regulations.

Finally, it is important to emphasize that companies' responsibility is not limited to mere regulatory compliance. Organizations must adopt a security culture that promotes awareness and ongoing education on cybersecurity topics. This includes regularly training employees about the risks associated with ransomware, warning signs, and emergency procedures.

In many countries, laws regarding ransom payments are still being developed, but there are already specific regulations that can influence the decision of companies. In the United States, for example, the government has taken a firm stance against paying ransoms to terrorist groups and criminal organizations. Executive Order 13773, signed in 2017, stipulated that companies should not pay ransoms, as this could further fuel criminal activity and make organizations vulnerable to future attacks. In addition, the Treasury Department has issued guidelines warning companies about the legal risks associated with paying ransoms, especially if funds are transferred to entities designated as terrorist.

At the state level, some laws impose severe restrictions on ransom payments. For example, in some states, companies could be persecuted if they pay a ransom to a group known for ties to criminal activity. This situation creates a dilemma for companies, which must balance the urgency of restoring access to data with the risk of legal penalties and moral responsibility not to fuel cybercrime.

In Europe, the situation is similar, although legislation varies from country to country. The European Union's position is clear: paying ransoms is not seen as a sustainable solution and can result in legal consequences. The GDPR, for example, does not have specific provisions on ransom payments, but it does require companies to protect personal data and take appropriate security measures. If a company decides to pay a ransom and fails to protect the data, later on, it could be held liable for violating data protection regulations.

In addition to existing regulations, companies must consider the ethical implications of a ransom payment. Paying a ransom can give the impression that a company is legitimizing criminal activity, contributing to a cycle of increasingly aggressive attacks. Furthermore, there is no guarantee that paying the ransom will actually lead to data restoration or the cessation of attacks. Some cybersecurity experts warn that paying may encourage further attacks, as criminals may perceive companies as easy targets.

In this context, it is crucial for companies to develop incident response plans that include clear protocols for handling ransomware attacks. These plans should include assessing the risks and legal consequences associated with paying a ransom. It is essential to involve legal and cybersecurity experts to guide the decision and evaluate the options available. In some cases, companies may find it helpful to contact law enforcement, who can offer support and resources to deal with the attack.

Organizations face the challenge of ensuring compliance with cybersecurity and data protection regulations. Implementing compliance protocols not only protects companies from legal penalties and reputational damage, but also helps to create a safer and more resilient work environment.

Compliance refers to compliance with relevant laws, regulations, and guidelines that govern data protection and cybersecurity. Regulations such as the General Data Protection Regulation (GDPR) in Europe, the California Consumer Privacy Act (CCPA) in the United States, and other national and international laws set specific requirements for organizations handling personal data. These requirements can vary greatly from one jurisdiction to another, creating complexity for companies operating globally. Therefore, creating clear and well-defined compliance protocols is essential to navigate this regulatory landscape.

One of the first steps in developing effective compliance protocols is to conduct a thorough analysis of applicable regulations. Companies need to identify which laws apply to their operations and the types of data they handle. This analysis should include reviewing data collection, storage, and processing practices, as well as assessing the associated risks. It is crucial to understand what rights individuals have regarding their data and what obligations companies have in protecting it.

Once the regulations are understood, companies must implement appropriate security measures to ensure compliance. This includes the adoption of data protection technologies such as encryption, firewalls, and intrusion detection systems. Additionally, it is essential to develop internal policies that dictate how data should be managed and protected. These policies should include guidelines on how to respond to security incidents, as well as processes for notifying data subjects and relevant authorities of breaches.

Continuous employee training is another crucial element of compliance protocols. Even the most advanced security measures can be ineffective if employees are not properly trained to recognize and manage the risks associated with cybersecurity. Companies need to invest in regular training programs that cover topics such as recognizing phishing emails, best practices for creating secure passwords, and procedures to follow in the event of a data breach. Creating a safety culture that actively engages all employees is key to reducing risk.

Additionally, companies should consider conducting regular compliance audits. These audits can help identify any gaps in security practices and internal policies, allowing organizations to make necessary changes before breaches occur. Audits should be conducted both internally and externally, with the participation of cybersecurity experts who can provide an unbiased assessment of the security measures taken.

Finally, it is crucial for companies to maintain comprehensive documentation of their compliance practices and the security measures they have taken. Not only does this documentation serve as proof of compliance in the event of audits or inspections, but it can also provide significant value in the event of legal litigation. Companies must be prepared to demonstrate that they have taken all necessary measures to protect personal data and that they have implemented adequate protocols to handle any breaches.

Implementing compliance protocols is essential for businesses looking to protect their data and comply with cybersecurity regulations. Through thorough regulatory analysis, taking appropriate safety measures, continuously training employees, and conducting regular audits, organizations can create a safe and resilient work environment.

Court cases and legal precedents have become increasingly relevant in defining companies' responsibilities and interpreting data protection regulations. We look at how courts have dealt with legal issues and the implications for companies and their approaches to cybersecurity.

One of the most emblematic cases is that of Target, the US retail giant, which suffered a data breach in 2013 that compromised the personal information of more than 40 million customers. While it was not a ransomware attack in the strict sense, the case had a significant impact on the legal perception of corporate cybersecurity responsibilities. Target has faced numerous lawsuits from customers and financial institutions that have suffered losses as a result of the breach. The court ruled that companies have an obligation to take reasonable steps to protect consumer data, and that negligence in doing so can result in legal liability. This case highlighted the importance of a robust cybersecurity strategy and prompted many companies to review their data protection practices.

Another significant example is the case of Anthem, one of the largest insurance companies in the United States, which suffered a cyberattack in 2015 that compromised the data of about 78 million people. In this case, Anthem was the subject of several class action lawsuits, and in 2017 it agreed to pay $115 million to compensate the customers and institutions involved. The courts have highlighted the responsibility of companies to adequately protect personal data and have ruled that paying a ransom does not exempt companies from legal responsibility for data protection. This case set an important precedent, pointing out that failure to protect data can have significant legal consequences, regardless of the measures taken after the attack.

A case of particular interest in the field of ransomware is that of the Cleveland Clinic, a major healthcare facility in the United States, which suffered a ransomware attack in 2017. In this case, cybercriminals blocked access to the data and demanded a ransom for recovery. Although Cleveland Clinic handled the attack without paying the ransom, the case raised questions related to liability for protecting patient data and led to a review of cybersecurity and crisis management policies. The courts have recognized that healthcare facilities have a special obligation to protect patients' health information and that any failure to do so could result in serious legal and reputational consequences.

In Europe, the case of British Airways was emblematic in relation to the GDPR. In 2018, the airline suffered a data breach that compromised the personal information of more than 500,000 customers. The UK Data Protection Authority has launched an investigation and proposed a £183 million fine, highlighting the responsibility of companies to protect consumer data. This case set an important precedent for GDPR enforcement, showing that regulators are ready to take action against companies that fail to comply with data protection obligations.

Another crucial aspect to consider is the role of insurance companies in managing the risks associated with ransomware attacks. Many companies have begun to take out cybersecurity-specific insurance policies, which can cover the costs associated with data breaches, ransom, and legal fees. However, recent legal cases have shown that insurance companies can deny coverage if the company has not taken reasonable security measures or if it has violated the conditions of the policy. This has led companies to reflect on the importance of compliance and preventive security measures.

Court cases and legal precedents related to ransomware attacks are shaping the landscape of corporate cybersecurity accountability. These cases highlight the importance of taking proactive measures to protect data and complying with applicable regulations. With the increasing attention of courts and regulators, companies must be ready to respond to legal challenges and ensure data security in an ever-changing environment. Investing in robust cybersecurity practices is not just a matter of compliance, but it is crucial to protect the reputation and sustainability of organizations in the long term.

Digital Epidemic

Ransoms and hostage data

Chapter 11

Prevention and IT Security

In today's environment, where cyber threats are evolving at a dizzying pace, ransomware is one of the most insidious pitfalls for businesses and individuals. This chapter aims to explore prevention and cybersecurity from an innovative perspective, going beyond traditional advice such as the need to make frequent backups and avoid opening suspicious attachments. Instead of limiting ourselves to these fundamental measures, we will dive into a holistic and proactive approach to security. We will explore how creating a culture of security within organizations, adopting emerging technologies, and collaborating across industries can provide an effective barrier against ransomware threats. Through an in-depth understanding of these aspects, we hope to equip readers with tools and knowledge to better protect their data and systems, contributing to a more secure and resilient digital environment.

Safety Culture

In today's digital landscape, where ransomware is a growing and evolving threat, prevention cannot be limited to technical solutions or reactive measures. A crucial element that is often overlooked is the safety culture within organizations. Creating an environment where all team members are aware and accountable about cybersecurity is critical to reducing the risk of attacks and ensuring an effective response in the event of a compromise. We will explore the importance of a safety culture, the strategies for promoting it, and the benefits that come with it.

Security culture refers to how an organization perceives and manages cybersecurity. It includes employees' attitudes, behaviors, and daily practices toward safety. When security is considered a priority by everyone, not just IT departments, it creates an environment where employees feel accountable and motivated to protect their data and the company's data.

A lack of awareness and training can lead to risky behavior, such as opening suspicious emails or using weak passwords. According to recent studies, a large proportion of ransomware attacks exploit human error, showing that a robust security culture is essential to mitigate such risks. It's not just about complying with regulations; It is a matter of building a real shield around sensitive data.

Regular training is key to maintaining awareness of cyber threats. Workshops, seminars, and online courses can educate employees on how to recognize threats and adopt safe practices. It is important that training is not an isolated event, but an ongoing process.

Management involvement: Leadership must be actively involved in promoting the safety culture. When executives demonstrate a commitment to safety, employees are more likely to follow their lead. Communications from above that emphasize the importance of safety can make a big difference.

Attack Simulations: Running phishing simulations and ransomware attacks can help employees recognize real-world situations. These tutorials not only test response skills, but also provide opportunities to learn and improve.

Feedback and Recognition: Creating an environment where employees feel free to report potential issues without fear of retaliation is vital. In addition, recognizing and rewarding virtuous behavior in the field of safety can encourage greater participation and attention.

Development of Clear Policies: It is essential for organizations to develop clear policies regarding cybersecurity and that these are easily accessible to all employees. Policies should clearly outline expectations, responsibilities, and procedures to be followed in the event of an accident.

Investing in creating a safety culture brings with it numerous benefits. In addition to reducing the risk of ransomware attacks, an environment where security is valued improves productivity and trust among team members. Employees who feel accountable for security tend to be more proactive and report potential threats, contributing to a safer work environment. Additionally, an effective security culture can improve the company's reputation. Customers and business partners are more likely to trust an organization that demonstrates a serious commitment to data protection. Creating a culture of security within organizations is not just a preventative measure, but a critical strategy for overall resilience. By investing in training, engaging leadership, and promoting clear and responsible practices, companies can build a strong defense against cyber threats. Security is not just the responsibility of the IT team; It is an issue that affects every single member of the organization. Only through a collective commitment will it be possible to effectively address the challenges of the future in the cybersecurity landscape.

Zero Trust Security Architecture: A New Frontier in Ransomware Protection

In the context of cybersecurity, the traditional paradigm of the "perimeter" is quickly becoming obsolete. With the rise of remote work, the use of personal devices, and the adoption of cloud services, the need for a more robust approach to security has become apparent. In this scenario, the Zero Trust security model emerges as an effective and necessary response, especially in the fight against ransomware. Let's explore the concept of Zero Trust architecture, its core principles, and how it can be implemented to improve cybersecurity in an increasingly connected world. Zero Trust is based on a key principle: "never trust, always verify." This approach means that no user or device, whether inside or outside the network, should be automatically trusted. Every access to resources must be authenticated and authorized, regardless of the user's location. This is especially crucial in the context of ransomware, as attackers often exploit stolen credentials to infiltrate corporate systems.

Strict Authentication and Authorization: Every access must be verified through robust authentication mechanisms, such as multi-factor authentication (MFA). This adds an extra layer of security, making it more difficult for attackers to gain unauthorized access.

Role-Based Access Control (RBAC): Permissions should only be granted based on the user's role and needs. This means that each employee will only have access to the information and systems they need to do their job, limiting exposure to sensitive data.

Continuous Monitoring and Analysis: Continuous vigilance is essential. Monitoring user activity and analyzing anomalous behavior helps identify potential breaches before they can cause significant damage.

Network Segmentation: Breaking the network into smaller segments can limit an attacker's ability to move laterally within the organization. Even if a device is compromised, segmentation prevents the entire network from being infected.

Assumption of Compromise: The Zero Trust model assumes that an attack may already be underway. This mindset encourages organizations to always be ready to respond to security incidents and implement mitigation measures.

Asset and Vulnerability Assessment: Before implementing a Zero Trust model, it is critical to conduct a thorough assessment of existing assets and potential vulnerabilities. Understanding which data and applications are most critical will help prioritize.

Adopt Advanced Security Technologies: The implementation of security solutions such as next-generation firewalls, intrusion prevention systems (IPS), and identity and access management (IAM) software is crucial to support Zero Trust.

Training and Awareness: Educating employees on Zero Trust principles and the importance of cybersecurity is essential for successful implementation. Training should include secure practices for accessing resources and managing credentials.

Testing and Simulations: Once the model is implemented, it is crucial to test its effectiveness through attack simulations and regular security audits. These activities help identify gaps and continuously improve security.

Continuous Evolution: Implementing Zero Trust is not a static process. Cyber threats evolve, and organizations must be ready to review and adapt their security strategies according to new emerging challenges.

There are many benefits to adopting a Zero Trust model. First, it significantly improves the organization's security posture, reducing the likelihood of breaches and ransomware attacks. In addition, continuous monitoring and data analysis enable a faster and more effective response to security incidents. Finally, network segmentation and strict access management can protect sensitive data and ensure compliance with current regulations. Investing in creating a Zero Trust environment not only reduces the risk of attacks, but also helps build a culture of security within the organization, where every member feels accountable for protecting data. In an increasingly connected world, adopting a Zero Trust mindset is essential to meet the challenges of the future.

Predictive Analytics and Artificial Intelligence: Innovations in the Fight Against Ransomware

The cybersecurity landscape is undergoing a radical transformation thanks to the adoption of advanced technologies such as predictive analytics and artificial intelligence (AI). Not only do these tools improve your threat detection capability, but they also provide an unprecedented opportunity to anticipate and prevent ransomware attacks before they can cause significant damage. This article will explore how predictive analytics and AI can be implemented to improve defenses against ransomware, the benefits they offer, and the challenges associated with their adoption. Predictive analytics uses historical data and advanced algorithms to predict future events. When applied to cybersecurity, this technology can identify anomalous behavior and patterns that could indicate an imminent attack. AI, on the other hand, allows systems to learn autonomously from data and continuously improve their detection and response capabilities. Both of these approaches are particularly relevant in the fight against ransomware, as attackers are becoming increasingly sophisticated, using techniques such as targeted phishing and polymorphic malware to evade traditional defenses. Using predictive analytics and AI allows you to take a proactive, rather than reactive, approach to data protection.

Data Collection and Analysis: To implement predictive analytics, organizations must first collect a large amount of data, including access logs, network events, and information about user behaviors. This data is then analyzed to identify patterns and anomalies.

Predictive Models: Using machine learning algorithms, data is processed to create predictive models that can identify potential threats. These patterns can recognize suspicious behavior that might go unnoticed by a human analysis.

Response Automation: AI can also automate responses to security incidents. For example, if abnormal behavior is detected, the system can automatically trigger containment measures, such as locking a device or logging out a suspicious user, reducing reaction time.

Continuous Improvement: A key aspect of AI is its ability to learn and improve over time. As the system collects more data and addresses new types of attacks, it can refine its defense models and strategies, becoming increasingly effective at detecting and preventing ransomware attacks.

Proactive Threat Detection: With the ability to analyze large volumes of data in real time, predictive analytics allows you to detect threats before they can cause damage. This proactive approach is crucial to prevent ransomware infections.

Rapid Incident Response: Response automation allows organizations to react quickly to potential threats, reducing the time it takes to contain and mitigate an attack.

Cost Reduction: Investing in predictive analytics and AI technologies can reduce the long-term costs associated with ransomware attacks. Preventing an attack is always less expensive than managing the consequences of an infection.

Adapting to New Threats: As attackers continually evolve their techniques, AI provides the flexibility to adapt to new attack patterns, ensuring that defenses remain effective over time.

Despite the many benefits, implementing predictive analytics and AI in cybersecurity also presents challenges. First of all, the quality of the data is crucial: inaccurate or incomplete data can lead to false positives or negatives, weakening the effectiveness of the system. Additionally, organizations must address the issue of privacy and regulatory compliance, ensuring that data analytics does not violate existing regulations.

Additionally, it is essential for organizations to invest in staff training to understand and manage these technologies. Without proper training, employees may not be able to correctly interpret the results and make informed decisions. Predictive analytics and artificial intelligence represent a paradigm shift in cybersecurity and offer a powerful tool in the fight against ransomware. With their ability to proactively detect threats, automate responses, and adapt to new attack techniques, these technologies are revolutionizing the way organizations protect their data. However, to fully exploit the potential of these innovations, it is crucial to address the challenges associated with their implementation and ensure that staff are properly trained. Investing in predictive analytics and AI is not just an option, but a necessity for companies looking to remain competitive and protected in a landscape increasingly threatened by cyberattacks.

Innovative Backup and Recovery: Advanced Strategies to Defend Against Ransomware

Having an effective backup and recovery plan is essential to ensure a company's resilience in the event of an attack. A solid backup plan is the first bulwark against ransomware. Attackers often encrypt victims' data, making it inaccessible, and demand a ransom for its restoration. If an organization has up-to-date and secure backups, it can avoid paying the ransom and restore its systems without significant data loss. However, not all backups are created equal. It is critical to adopt backup strategies that ensure the security, integrity, and accessibility of your data. Below are some of the best practices and innovative technologies for backup and recovery.

Immutable backups are one of the most effective methods of protecting backups from ransomware is the use of immutable backups. These backups are designed in such a way that once created, they cannot be modified or deleted. This means that even if an attacker manages to infiltrate the system, they will not be able to access immutable backups to encrypt or delete them. This technology is crucial to ensure the availability of data in the event of an attack.

Adopting the "3-2-1" strategy for backups is a proven approach. This strategy involves having three copies of the data, on two different types of media, with one copy stored off-site. Not only does this approach offer robust protection against data loss, but it also ensures that backups are available in different physical locations, reducing the risk of loss due to physical disasters or targeted attacks.

Using cloud-based backup solutions offers numerous benefits, including scalability, accessibility, and cost reduction. Hybrid architectures, which combine local and cloud backup, allow organizations to maintain control over critical data while benefiting from the security and reliability of cloud solutions. Additionally, the cloud can provide disaster recovery options that can be activated quickly in the event of an attack.

Incremental and differential backups are techniques that can significantly reduce the time and storage space required. Incremental backups save only the changes made from previous backups, while differential backups retain all changes since the last full backup. These techniques not only speed up the backup process but also make it easier to restore data in the event of a ransomware attack.

Having an effective backup plan is not enough; It is crucial to test the recovery process regularly. Organizations should run recovery simulations to ensure that data can be restored quickly and completely. These tests help identify any gaps in the backup plan and ensure that personnel are trained to handle the recovery process in the event of a disaster.

Encrypting backup data is an additional method of protecting sensitive information. Encrypting data ensures that even if an attacker manages to gain access to backups, they won't be able to read or use the information. Implementing robust encryption techniques is therefore essential to ensure the confidentiality and integrity of your data.

Implementing monitoring systems for backups allows organizations to detect suspicious activity and anomalies in the backup process. Timely notifications can help identify an ongoing attack and take preventative measures before the damage spreads. This continuous vigilance is a key component of an integrated security strategy.

Post-Incident Analysis: Learning to Improve Security Against Ransomware

Post-incident analysis is a crucial process that allows companies to learn from adverse security events, improve their protective measures, and strengthen overall resilience. This article will explore the importance of post-incident analysis, its key steps, and how it can contribute to a more robust cybersecurity strategy.

Post-incident analysis is essential to understand how an attack occurred, what vulnerabilities were exploited, and what steps may have been taken to prevent the incident. Not only does this process help improve security, but it also provides an opportunity to review and update existing security policies and practices.

In addition, post-incident analysis helps create a culture of security within the organization, where every employee is aware of the importance of data protection and the need to learn from mistakes. Finally, a good post-incident analysis helps maintain regulatory compliance and protect the company's reputation.

Basic Steps of Post-Incident Analysis

Information Collection: The first step in post-incident analysis is to gather all relevant information regarding the incident. This includes system logs, network monitoring reports, employee testimonials, and any other evidence that can help reconstruct the sequence of events. It's critical that this step happens promptly, as data can quickly become outdated or difficult to obtain.

Root Cause Identification: Once the information has been gathered, the next step is to identify the root causes of the incident. This involves a thorough analysis to understand how and why the attack occurred. Techniques such as weakness analysis, event analysis, and creating cause-and-effect diagrams can be used to facilitate this process.

Impact Assessment: It is important to assess the impact of the incident on the organization. This includes quantifying economic losses, assessing legal consequences, and considering the impact on customer and stakeholder trust. A thorough impact analysis will help justify future spending on security improvements.

Documentation and Reporting: All analysis results must be documented in a clear and detailed manner. This report should include the root causes identified, the impact assessed, and recommendations for future improvements. Documentation is essential not only for internal analysis but also for any external audits or legal investigations.

Development of Recommendations and Action Plans: Based on the conclusions of the analysis, it is crucial to develop concrete recommendations to improve safety. These action plans must be specific, measurable, and actionable, and should include deadlines and responsibilities assigned for each task.

Implementation of Improvement Measures: Once action plans have been defined, it is important to implement corrective measures quickly.

This could include updating security policies, training staff on new security practices, and adopting advanced technologies to prevent future attacks.

Monitoring and Review: After corrective measures have been implemented, it is crucial to continuously monitor and review the effectiveness of new security practices. This can include regular security audits, penetration testing, and attack simulations to ensure that the measures taken are sufficient to protect the organization.

Post-incident analysis offers numerous advantages. First of all, it helps organizations better understand their vulnerabilities and strengthen their defenses. It also allows you to learn from your mistakes, reducing the risk of future accidents. Documentation and reporting can also facilitate regulatory compliance and improve the company's reputation, demonstrating a proactive commitment to data protection.

In addition, post-incident analysis fosters a culture of security within the organization, encouraging employees to be more aware of cyber threats and actively participate in protecting corporate data.

Security for Remote Work: Protecting Data in the Digital Age

With the rise of remote work, accelerated by the COVID-19 pandemic, cybersecurity has become a primary concern for organizations around the world. While working from home offers flexibility and opportunities, it also brings with it new security challenges, particularly when it comes to protecting sensitive data and preventing ransomware attacks. We'll look at best practices for ensuring safety while working remotely, highlighting the importance of effective policies, advanced technology, and ongoing employee training.

The Challenges of Security in Remote Work

Employees who work from home may use home Wi-Fi networks that are not protected with the same security measures as corporate networks. This increases the risk of eavesdropping and attacks. Many employees use personal devices to access company information. These devices may not have up-to-date security software or proper configurations.

Phishing and Targeted Attacks: Attackers can leverage remote work to send more targeted phishing emails, taking advantage of employees' diminished attention span or vulnerability due to the situation.

Monitoring Difficulty: Monitoring activity on remote devices can be more complex than in a traditional work environment, making it difficult to detect suspicious behavior in real time.

Using VPNs (Virtual Private Networks): Using a VPN allows employees to securely connect to the corporate network, encrypting transmitted data and protecting information from potential eavesdropping. It's crucial that all business communication takes place through a VPN to ensure security.

Multi-factor authentication (MFA): Implementing multi-factor authentication for access to corporate systems is one of the most effective measures to protect accounts. This approach requires users to provide more than one verification method, such as a password and a code sent to their phone, thus increasing access security.

Clear Security Policies: It is essential to develop and communicate clear security policies for remote work. These policies should detail expectations for device use, password management, access to corporate data, and procedures to be followed if a breach is suspected.

Regular Updates and Patches: Devices used for remote work should be regularly updated with the latest security patches. This includes operating systems, application software, and security tools.

Organizations should provide clear guidelines on how and when to perform these updates.

Use of Security Software: Make sure that all devices used for remote work are equipped with up-to-date antivirus and antispyware software. These tools can detect and prevent malware and ransomware attacks, protecting corporate data.

Limited Data Access: Implement the principle of "least privilege" to limit access to sensitive data to only those employees who really need it. This reduces the risk of accidental or intentional exposure of confidential information.

Data Backup: Ensure that data is regularly backed up, whether it is stored locally or in the cloud. An effective backup plan allows you to quickly restore your data in the event of a ransomware attack or data loss.

Monitoring and Auditing: Implement monitoring systems to detect suspicious activity on remote devices. Regular audits can help identify any vulnerabilities and ensure that security policies are being adhered to.

Digital Epidemic
Ransoms and hostage data

Chapter 12

The Technical Functioning of an Antivirus

to Detect Ransomware

Traditional detection methods, based on signatures of known viruses, continue to play an important role, behavioral analysis is emerging as a key strategy to combat these forms of malware. We will explore in detail how behavior analysis works, its benefits, and the challenges it presents.

Behavioral analysis is a cybersecurity technique that focuses on monitoring and analyzing the actions and behaviors of software running on a system. Unlike traditional methods that rely on predefined malware signatures, behavioral analysis seeks to identify suspicious activity based on patterns of anomalous behavior. This approach allows you to detect threats that have not yet been cataloged, including next-generation ransomware that uses techniques to evade traditional defenses.

Behavioral analysis is based on machine learning and artificial intelligence algorithms. These algorithms are trained on massive volumes of data, which include both legitimate activity and malicious behavior. Through this learning process, the system is able to build "normal" behavior profiles for a wide variety of applications and processes.

When a file or program is executed, the antivirus starts monitoring its actions. If the software begins to perform unusual actions, such as encrypting files on disk, attempting to access protected directories, or communicating with external servers in unauthorized ways, the system may treat these activities as indicators of a potential ransomware attack. Behavioral analysis is particularly effective against ransomware, as these programs tend to exhibit characteristic behaviors that can be identified, even if the software itself has never been seen before.

One of the main benefits of behavioral analytics is its ability to detect unknown threats. Unlike signature-based systems, which can fail to recognize new or modified variants of malware, behavioral analysis can identify malicious activity based on how a piece of software behaves, rather than what it is. This proactive approach allows for a faster and more targeted response to potential threats. Additionally, behavioral analysis can reduce false positives. Because the system can distinguish between normal and suspicious activity, it is less likely to falsely flag a legitimate application as malicious, which is a common problem in signature-based systems. Despite its many benefits, behavioral analysis also presents some challenges. One of the main obstacles is the complexity of human behavior and normal business processes. In a work environment, seemingly harmless activities might be interpreted as suspicious. Therefore, the accuracy of the analysis must be constantly refined and improved. Furthermore, cybercriminals are always one step ahead and may try to disguise their activities to evade behavioral detection. This leads to an ongoing war between security software developers and hackers, where each side tries to outdo the other. Behavioral analytics represents a promising frontier in the fight against ransomware and other cyber threats. With its ability to identify anomalous behavior and detect unknown threats, it offers a more dynamic and responsive approach than traditional signature-based methods. However, the challenges related to the complexity of human behavior and the continuous evolution of attack techniques require constant updating and improvement of technology. In this context, behavioral analysis is not only a powerful defense tool, but also a crucial element in building an increasingly robust cybersecurity ecosystem.

Sandboxing: A Security Beacon in Ransomware Detection

Sandboxing is a cybersecurity technique that allows suspicious applications or files to be executed in an isolated environment, known as a "sandbox." This simulated environment is separate from the main operating system and other resources, allowing software to be tested without the risk of infecting the system. It's like a "protective bubble" where experiments can take place without detrimental consequences for the rest of the infrastructure.

When a file or application runs in a sandbox, security software can closely monitor its actions. If the behavior is suspicious or malicious, the system can step in and block execution before the software can cause any real damage. The sandboxing process begins with the identification of a suspicious file or application. When the user tries to open a file that is not recognized or downloaded from an untrusted source, the antivirus software must decide whether the file may pose a threat. Instead of immediately running the file on the main system, the software transfers it to a sandbox. Within the sandbox, the file runs in a controlled environment. Here, security software can monitor the file's behavior, observing its interactions with the system, changes made to files, and network calls made. If the program attempts to encrypt files, access protected information, or communicate with external servers, the system recognizes these actions as suspicious activity and can take action. One of the main benefits of sandboxing is the ability to detect unknown malware. As cybercriminals continually develop new ransomware variants, signature-based methods may not be enough to prevent attacks. Sandboxing allows users to test suspicious files without risk of exposure, allowing for accurate threat assessment. In addition, sandboxing reduces the risk of false positives. Many legitimate files or applications can trigger alarms in traditional antivirus systems, but within a sandbox, a file's behavior can be analyzed more accurately. If the file does not exhibit malicious behavior, it can be allowed to run on the main system without worry. An added benefit is that sandboxing can serve as a post-incident analysis tool. In the event that a malicious file manages to infiltrate the system, analyzing its actions within the sandbox can provide valuable information about how the infection occurred and which vulnerabilities were exploited.

However, sandboxing is not without its challenges. One of the main limitations is that not all malware can be effectively detected in a sandbox. Some ransomware is designed to recognize if it is in an isolated environment and can change its behavior accordingly, or it can delay the malicious action until after it has been executed in the same environment. This ability to adapt makes it difficult to detect some threats early. Additionally, sandboxing requires significant resources, both in terms of processing power and storage. Creating and managing sandboxes can be expensive, especially for organizations that need to test a large number of files and applications on a daily basis.

Implementing sandboxing requires some technical expertise. Organizations must ensure that their staff are properly trained to manage and interpret the results of analyses conducted within sandboxes. Without the right knowledge, the benefits of sandboxing may not be fully realized.

Detecting by Clues: Deciphering Ransomware Signals

To effectively counter ransomware, it is crucial to develop advanced detection techniques. Among these, detection by clues proves to be a promising strategy, as it is based on the analysis of digital and behavioral signals rather than the simple identification of malware signatures.

Clue detection is an approach to cybersecurity that relies on observing anomalous signals and behavior within a system. Instead of relying solely on predefined malware signatures, this method considers a variety of indicators that may suggest the presence of ransomware or other threats. These clues can include unusual behavior, file changes, suspicious network activity, or even glitches in system processes.

The process of detecting clues begins with collecting and analyzing data from different sources. Antivirus and security systems constantly monitor activity within the system, collecting information about disk read and write operations, directory access, network communications, and more. This data is then processed to identify patterns or anomalies that could indicate an ongoing ransomware attack.

Some examples of clues that can be tracked include:

Quick File Changes: Ransomware often encrypts files massively and quickly. If an application tries to access and modify a large number of files in a short amount of time, it could be a warning sign.

Access to Protected Directories: Attempting to access system directories or sensitive files can indicate malicious behavior, especially if the access is from applications that would not normally have these permissions.

Suspicious Network Activity: Many ransomware communicates with external servers to receive instructions or to send encrypted data. Monitoring network traffic for unauthorized or unusual connections can provide additional clues about the presence of malware.

Changes in File Extensions: Known ransomware tends to modify the extensions of encrypted files. If a large number of files change extension in a short period, this could be a key indicator of an ongoing infection.

Signals from Security Software: Alerts generated by security software, such as unauthorized access attempts or network scanning activities, can serve as crucial clues in identifying an attack.

One of the main benefits of detecting through clues is its ability to identify new and unknown threats. Because it doesn't rely solely on malware signatures, this approach can detect ransomware variants that haven't been cataloged yet. Additionally, detection through clues can provide a more comprehensive view of system activity, allowing for a faster and more targeted response to threats. Another positive aspect is that this method allows you to reduce false positives. Because it relies on specific indicators and suspicious behavior, it is less likely to incorrectly flag legitimate applications as malicious. This is especially important in enterprise environments, where operational disruptions can have significant consequences. However, detecting by clues also presents several challenges. First, collecting and analyzing real-time data requires significant resources. Organizations must ensure that their systems can handle large volumes of data and process it quickly to identify threats in time. In addition, cybercriminals are increasingly adept at avoiding detection. They may use techniques to mask their behavior, such as encrypting data in a stepwise manner or using obfuscation techniques to hide their activities. This makes it even more difficult to detect threats early and accurately. Interpreting clues can be complex. Not all abnormal signs are necessarily indicative of a ransomware attack. Therefore, it is crucial that security analysts are properly trained to distinguish between normal and suspicious behavior, thus avoiding false alarms or, worse, underestimation of a real threat.

Detecting by clues is an innovative and dynamic approach in the fight against ransomware. By analyzing behavioral and digital signals, this method offers a more proactive and informed response to cyber threats. Despite the associated challenges, such as the need for significant resources and the increasing sophistication of attack techniques, detection by clues continues to be a crucial element in cybersecurity strategies. As threats continue to evolve, taking a clue-based approach can make all the difference in protecting your data and business operations.

Future of Ransomware Detection: Innovations and Perspectives

One of the most promising innovations in the field of ransomware detection is the integration of artificial intelligence (AI) and machine learning (ML). These technologies can analyze massive amounts of data to identify anomalous patterns and behaviors that may be missed by human analysis. Machine learning algorithms can be trained on datasets that include both legitimate activity and previous attacks, allowing them to learn which behaviors are considered normal and which are potentially harmful. This approach not only improves the detection of known ransomware, but also allows it to identify emerging variants that may not have specific virus signatures. Additionally, AI can facilitate automated incident response, allowing systems to neutralize threats in real-time. This speed of intervention is crucial, as ransomware can spread quickly within a network, causing significant damage in a matter of hours. The future of ransomware detection will also require greater collaboration between organizations. Threat databases and information-sharing platforms become essential in improving threat awareness and accelerating response to attacks. By sharing information about attack techniques, vulnerabilities, and malware samples, companies can collaborate to strengthen their defenses. This way, when new ransomware emerges, information can be spread quickly, allowing all members of the security community to take effective countermeasures.

Another crucial aspect for the future of ransomware detection is user education. Many ransomware attacks start with user manipulation, such as phishing or social engineering. Therefore, proper cybersecurity training can significantly reduce the risk of infection.

Finally, emerging technologies, such as blockchain, could offer innovative solutions to improve security against ransomware. Due to its decentralized and immutable nature, blockchain could be used to track and verify data transactions, making it more difficult for cybercriminals to compromise systems. Using blockchain to ensure data integrity could provide an extra layer of security. For example, if encrypted files were recorded on a blockchain, it would be possible to verify their authenticity and prevent unauthorized changes.

Digital Epidemic

Ransoms and hostage data

Chapter 13

Ransomware and Industrial Espionage

In the digital age we live in, cybersecurity has become a top priority for businesses in every industry. Among the various threats looming, ransomware and industrial espionage emerge as two of the most insidious and devastating. Although they may seem distinct phenomena, a thorough analysis reveals that there is a worrying intersection between them, where ransomware is not only a means of extorting money, but also a strategic tool for stealing sensitive data and confidential information. These types of attacks have evolved over time, with cybercriminals honing their techniques to target companies' vulnerabilities in increasingly sophisticated ways. Traditionally, attackers focus on economic extortion; However, recent developments have revealed an additional dimension: the use of ransomware as a vehicle for stealing critical information.

Industrial espionage, on the other hand, is an illegal practice that involves the theft of trade secrets and confidential information by competitors or state actors. Targets can range from patents and chemical formulas to market strategies and customer data. In a highly competitive environment, access to such information can provide a decisive advantage, motivating attackers to resort to increasingly daring methods to obtain it.

The intersection of ransomware and industrial espionage manifests itself when cybercriminals use ransomware to mask data theft. In this scenario, the attacker does not just encrypt the data but also extracts it to then resell it or use it for competitive purposes. In fact, ransomware can serve as a strategic "distraction": while the company's attention is focused on recovering data and paying the ransom, the most critical data is stolen. There have been documented cases where companies have suffered ransomware attacks that have revealed sensitive information. For example, the case of a large tech company that, after paying a ransom, discovered that its R&D projects had been stolen and sold to competitors. Not only did this result in an immediate financial loss, but it also inflicted irreparable damage on the company's reputation.

Cybercriminals have developed sophisticated techniques to carry out targeted ransomware attacks. By using social engineering to trick employees and infiltrate company systems, they can gather valuable information before launching the attack. In addition, advanced tools such as botnets and malware as a service make the attack more accessible even to those without high technical skills.

Combining ransomware with industrial espionage requires a more complex and nuanced approach to cybersecurity. Businesses must not only worry about preventing ransoms from being paid, but also about protecting their most critical data from unauthorized access. To address this dual threat, companies must take proactive and reactive measures. It is crucial to implement an integrated cybersecurity strategy that includes employee training, regularly updating security systems, and adopting advanced intrusion detection technologies. In addition, you need to have a well-defined incident response plan that covers not only data recovery, but also communication management and protection of sensitive information.

The intersection of ransomware and industrial espionage represents a new threat paradigm in the cybersecurity landscape. Companies must recognize that defense against ransomware cannot be limited to preventing ransoms from being paid, but must extend to protecting critical information. Only through a holistic and integrated approach to cybersecurity will it be possible to effectively address these emerging threats and safeguard the future of organizations.

Case Studies: Ransomware and Industrial Espionage – Lessons from Real-World Attacks

Ransomware and industrial espionage are crippling threats that, in recent years, have affected an increasing number of companies around the world. Real-world attack case studies offer important learnings about vulnerabilities, attack strategies, and defense best practices. In this article, we will look at some emblematic cases where ransomware has acted as an industrial espionage tool, analyzing companies' responses and lessons learned.

Case 1: Attack on Garmin

In July 2020, Garmin, a tech giant in the shipping and fitness industries, suffered a ransomware attack that had devastating impacts. The attackers, belonging to the Evil Corp group, blocked access to the company's systems and demanded a ransom of about $10 million. In addition to the shutdown of services, the attack led to the loss of crucial data related to customers and business operations.

One of the main concerns was the theft of data related to users' health, which is extremely sensitive information in the current context. Garmin has faced not only immediate economic impact, but also reputational damage that could affect consumer confidence in the long term. The main lesson from this case is the importance of having an incident response plan that is not just limited to recovery, but also considers the protection of sensitive data.

Case 2: Attack on Colonial Pipeline

Another significant case study is that of Colonial Pipeline, one of the largest oil transportation infrastructures in the United States. In May 2021, the company was hit by ransomware that led to the temporary closure of a significant portion of the distribution network. The attackers, the DarkSide group, demanded a ransom of $4.4 million, which Colonial Pipeline paid to restore services.

However, the attack exposed not only vulnerabilities in the energy sector, but also how ransomware can be used to affect national security. The attack raised concerns about the possibility of similar attacks in the future, potentially targeting sensitive data or critical infrastructure. From this case, companies should learn the importance of assessing not only the immediate risks related to ransomware, but also the long-term consequences on security and operational stability.

Case 3: Attack on Mitsubishi Electric

In January 2021, Mitsubishi Electric, a Japanese tech giant, suffered a ransomware attack that compromised the data of thousands of employees and customers. The attackers managed to infiltrate the company's systems, stealing sensitive information and demanding a ransom. The case raised concerns about the protection of sensitive information and highlighted existing vulnerabilities in the security systems of large companies. Analysis of this attack shows how crucial it is for companies to take proactive security measures, such as regular system audits and ongoing employee training on cybersecurity. In particular, employee awareness of social engineering practices can significantly reduce the risk of attacks.

Case 4: Attack on JBS Foods

In May 2021, JBS Foods, one of the world's largest meat producers, was hit by a ransomware attack that forced the company to temporarily close some production facilities. The attackers, also part of the REvil group, demanded a ransom of $11 million. The attack had significant repercussions on the food supply chain, highlighting how ransomware can affect not only individual companies, but also the entire economic ecosystem.

The key takeaway from this attack is the importance of integrated and coordinated security management between different parts of the company and suppliers. An attack on a single link in the supply chain can have knock-on effects across the industry.

The analysis of these case studies highlights the complexity of the threats posed by ransomware and industrial espionage. Companies need to recognize that data protection is not just a cybersecurity issue, but a crucial element of their overall business strategy.

Emerging technologies will play a crucial role in shaping the future of ransomware and industrial espionage attacks. Some of the key technologies to consider include:

Blockchain: Although initially conceived for transaction security, blockchain technology could also be used to improve data security and create immutable records of transactions. However, criminals could exploit blockchain to make it more difficult to track ransom payments.

Internet of Things (IoT): The rise of IoT devices in enterprises opens up new frontiers for attackers. Every connected device represents a potential entry point into corporate systems, increasing the risk of ransomware attacks and espionage.

5G and advanced connectivity: As the 5G network expands, the speed and efficiency of communication will increase, but this could also facilitate faster and more coordinated attacks. Attack groups could take advantage of the increased connectivity to launch large-scale, real-time attacks.

Digital Epidemic

Ransoms and hostage data

Chapter 14

The Dark Web

In recent years, ransomware has emerged as one of the most lucrative and devastating cyber threats, affecting businesses, government organizations, and individuals around the world. But behind these attacks lies an even more disturbing phenomenon: the ransomware market on the Dark Web. This chapter will explore how the Dark Web has created a fertile environment for ransomware proliferation, examining market dynamics, business practices, and cybersecurity implications.

The Dark Web, a part of the internet that is not indexed and can only be accessed through specific software such as Tor, has created an underground market where cybercriminals can trade illicit goods and services. Among them, ransomware has found a prominent place. The ransomware market is estimated to have generated billions of dollars in ransoms, making it a highly lucrative business for criminals.

Dark Web marketplaces operate similarly to legitimate ones, with product catalogs, secure payment systems, and review mechanisms. Here, criminals can purchase various types of ransomware, some of which are ready-to-use, while others offer customizable features to suit the buyer's specific needs. This "out-of-the-box" approach is a key driver of the rise in ransomware, as it allows anyone, even without technical skills, to launch cyberattacks.

The price of ransomware on the Dark Web can vary greatly. Some packages can cost a few hundred dollars, while more sophisticated ransomware can cost in the thousands. User reviews and word-of-mouth play a crucial role in this market. Cybercriminals often leave feedback on various ransomware tools, creating a sort of ranking that guides purchasing decisions.

In addition, many sellers offer promotions and discounts to attract new customers, further incentivizing the spread of these malicious technologies. Some marketplaces have even implemented affiliate

109

programs, allowing ransomware buyers to earn a commission on ransoms paid by victims.

The Role of Support and Assistance

A surprising aspect of the ransomware market is the presence of technical support for buyers. Vendors offer assistance with malware installation and configuration, as well as after-sales support to help hackers maximize their profits. This service may include detailed tutorials on how to launch attacks, manage communications with victims, and ultimately cash ransoms. This support infrastructure makes ransomware accessible even to those with poor IT skills, democratizing access to technologies that were once reserved for skilled hackers. The proliferation of ransomware on the Dark Web has serious consequences for victims.

The Dark Web is a dark and mysterious place, a corner of the Internet where lawlessness thrives and where stolen data becomes a bargaining chip. In recent years, the market for stolen data has seen an unprecedented explosion, fueled by ransomware attacks and other forms of cybercrime. We will explore how stolen data is sold, exchanged, and used on the Dark Web, analyzing the implications for cybersecurity and the lives of individuals.

In the Dark Web landscape, stolen data is invaluable. Personal information, such as Social Security numbers, banking credentials, and credit card information, are sold at prices ranging from a few dollars to thousands, depending on their quality and rarity. For example, a data package that includes complete information about an individual – name, address, phone number, email, and financial data – can reach high figures, making cyberattacks a potentially very lucrative investment for hackers.

Another highly sought-after category of stolen data is that of access credentials to corporate accounts. Businesses, in particular, are attractive targets for cybercriminals, as their data can provide access to valuable and sensitive resources. Stolen login credentials can be sold to third parties, used to carry out targeted attacks, or simply to extort money from victims.

The market for stolen data on the Dark Web operates similarly to a traditional market, with platforms that facilitate the buying and selling of information. These platforms can range from discussion forums to full-fledged marketplaces, where users can explore catalogs of available data and evaluate offers. The payment methods used on the Dark Web, mainly cryptocurrencies such as Bitcoin and Monero, guarantee a degree of anonymity and make it difficult to trace transactions. This anonymity is crucial for criminals, as it protects their identities and illicit operations from possible investigation.

A crucial aspect of the stolen data market is its connection to ransomware attacks. Many hacking groups not only encrypt their victims' data and demand a ransom, but they also collect sensitive information in the process. This data can then be sold on the Dark Web, creating a double source of profit for criminals. Victims, therefore, not only face ransom, but also risk having their personal information disseminated to a wider audience.

The increase in the market for stolen data poses a significant threat to cybersecurity. Businesses and individuals face the risk of identity theft, financial fraud, and privacy breaches.

The Dark Web is a constantly changing ecosystem, a place where innovation is not only a feature of technological progress, but also a phenomenon of adaptation to the needs and challenges of cybercrime. In this context, ransomware has evolved rapidly, with hacker groups experimenting with new techniques and strategies to maximize their profits and overcome security countermeasures. We will see how experimentation and innovation on the Dark Web have contributed to the evolution of ransomware, making it an increasingly sophisticated and pervasive threat.

On the Dark Web, experimentation is the order of the day. Hacking groups don't just use standard attack techniques, they're continually looking for ways to improve the effectiveness of their ransomware. Some of the most significant innovations include:

Strong Encryption: Many ransomware groups have begun to implement more complex encryption algorithms, making it more difficult for victims to restore their data without paying the ransom. Techniques such as public-key cryptography have become increasingly common, increasing the level of security for criminals.

Targeted and Customized Attacks: With the increased availability of data on the Dark Web, ransomware groups can now conduct targeted attacks, selecting specific companies or individuals based on the potential value of their data. This personalized approach increases the likelihood of success and the chance of higher redemptions. The fight against ransomware requires global cooperation between law enforcement and cybersecurity agencies. Information exchange and joint action are essential to address the transnational nature of cybercrime.

Digital Epidemic
Ransoms and hostage data

Chapter 15

The Power of Distance: Psychology of Ranged Damage

As news of serious cyberattacks rolls in, a psychological phenomenon emerges that deserves attention: the effect of distance on our ability to feel empathy for victims. This chapter will explore how physical and temporal distance can influence indifference to the damage caused by ransomware, analyzing psychological experiments and practical implications.

Distance, whether physical or psychological, plays a crucial role in how we perceive the pain and suffering of others. Studies show that when people are not directly exposed to traumatic events, they tend to feel less involved and less motivated to act. This phenomenon is known as "empathic indifference," a condition in which the suffering of someone who is far away from us is perceived as less meaningful.

In a context of ransomware, victims of these attacks may seem abstract or distant. When a large company is hit, the news can make headlines, but individuals often fail to connect emotionally with the employees or customers who suffer the consequences. The absence of a personal connection reduces the drive to show empathy or take preventive measures. An experiment conducted by psychologists showed that people are significantly more likely to donate to a cause if they can see and hear a victim's story directly. For example, when presented with a single story of a sick child, people tend to donate higher sums than when presented with a statistic describing a disease that affects many children. This phenomenon is known as the "individual effect," which highlights how personal connection can activate stronger empathic responses. Applying this concept to ransomware, it can be observed that when victims are presented as individual stories, the public's reaction is often more intense. However, when the damage is described in general terms or as part of a statistic, the emotional response tends to decrease. This dynamic can contribute to a lack of preparedness and awareness of the real risks that ransomware presents.

The media plays a vital role in shaping our perception of ransomware attacks and their victims. News stories that focus on personal stories, such as those of small businesses affected or individuals who have lost valuable data, can evoke a stronger empathetic response than general reports of attacks on large companies. However, the focus is often on statistics and numbers, which can create an emotional distance between the reader and the victim. Additionally, the depiction of ransomware attacks in movies and popular culture can amplify this indifference. When cybercrime is described as a spectacular and dramatic event, the public may perceive it as an adventurous action rather than a real, concrete threat. This can lead to an underestimation of risks and a failure to activate the empathic reaction.

The lack of empathy towards ransomware victims has significant implications for preventing and responding to these attacks. If people do not perceive the damage as real or close to them, they may be less likely to take appropriate precautions, such as adopting cybersecurity practices or training to recognize potential attacks. To address this indifference, it's critical to change the way we communicate and present stories related to ransomware attacks. Educating audiences not only through data and statistics, but also through human narratives that highlight the real impact of such events, can help reduce emotional distance and promote greater empathy.

Desensitization and Normalization: Ransomware in the Collective Perception

In recent years, the frequency and variety of ransomware attacks have increased exponentially, making these events a sad normality in the daily lives of individuals and organizations. However, this increase has led to a worrying phenomenon: the desensitization of the public to these threats. This article examines the process of desensitization and normalization in relation to ransomware, exploring how these phenomena affect our perception of risk, preventive behavior, and emotional reactions.

Desensitization is a psychological process in which repeated exposure to a traumatic event or negative situation leads to a decrease in emotional reaction. In the context of ransomware attacks, constant exposure to news regarding data breaches, digital extortion, and attacks on large companies has led many people to consider these threats as ordinary and not exceptional events. Psychological studies have shown that when people are exposed to images or stories of violence or suffering, their emotional response tends to diminish with time. This phenomenon is particularly relevant in the field of cybersecurity, where overexposure to news about ransomware attacks can lead to a distorted perception of real risk, making these events appear inevitable and common.

Normalization is the process by which a behavior or event, initially considered abnormal or worrying, becomes accepted as part of the daily routine. In the case of ransomware, the normalization of risk can be alarming. While data breaches were perceived as serious exceptions in the past, today many see attacks as an inevitable aspect of digital life. This change in perception can have significant consequences. As individuals and organizations begin to view ransomware attacks as a "part of the game," they may become less likely to invest in security measures, such as adopting protection software, data backups, and staff training. Normalizing risk creates a false sense of security, leading to increasing vulnerability.

The media play a crucial role in the process of desensitization and normalization. Constant coverage of ransomware attacks, often accompanied by alarming statistics, can contribute to a sense of helplessness and, paradoxically, a decrease in emotional reaction. When audiences are bombarded with news about breaches and attacks, stories lose their novelty and emotional impact. In addition, the tendency to treat ransomware attacks as spectacular or dramatic events can reduce the perception of real risk. The depiction of attacks in movies and media can help create a distorted picture of cybercrime, making hackers appear as adventurous protagonists rather than actual security threats.

The desensitization and normalization of risk related to ransomware attacks have significant implications for cybersecurity. Organizations, due to this decrease in emotional responsiveness, can fall into the trap of complacency, losing sight of the importance of adequate preventive measures. This can lead to devastating consequences, not only in terms of financial damage, but also in terms of loss of customer trust and reputational damage.

To counter these phenomena, a shift is needed in the way we communicate and discuss ransomware attacks. Awareness campaigns should aim to emotionally engage the public, using personal stories and testimonies of victims to recover the emotional impact and reduce indifference. Creating a narrative that highlights the real, human damage caused by attacks can help promote greater awareness and accountability.

Conclusion

In an age where digitalization permeates every aspect of our daily lives, cybersecurity is no longer just a technical issue, but a collective imperative. The lessons learned through the pages of this book remind us that each of us has a critical role to play in protecting our data and systems. Whether we are private citizens, professionals within a company or responsible parents, it is essential to take all the necessary precautions to safeguard the information and safety of the people around us. For individuals, adopting security practices such as using strong passwords, enabling two-factor authentication, and vigilance against online scams are key steps in protecting their digital assets. Every individual needs to become aware of the threats that exist and the need to stay informed about the latest trends in cybersecurity. For companies, responsibility is amplified. It is imperative to implement robust security policies, provide ongoing training to employees, and maintain an open dialogue about cybersecurity. Creating a company culture that values security not only protects company data, but also strengthens customer and stakeholder trust. Finally, as parents, we have the crucial task of educating our children about the importance of online safety. Teaching them to navigate safely, recognize dangers, and protect their personal information is crucial to preparing future generations to live in an increasingly complex digital world. In conclusion, cybersecurity is a shared responsibility that requires attention and commitment from all of us. Investing time and energy in training and awareness is essential to building a safer digital environment. Only through a collective effort can we hope to meet future challenges and protect our data and privacy in an ever-changing world. The security of our IT systems is key to ensuring a safer and more resilient future for all.

In writing this book on ransomware, I have referred to a number of authoritative sources that have helped to paint a complete and detailed picture of this complex and ever-evolving phenomenon. My research focused not only on the historical data and technical aspects of ransomware attacks, but also on their psychological implications and economic consequences for victims.

One of the key texts I consulted is "Security Engineering: A Guide to Building Dependable Distributed Systems" by Ross Anderson. This book offers an in-depth look at the basics of cybersecurity and provides essential historical context for understanding the evolution of threats, including ransomware. Anderson's theories and principles were a starting point for my exploration of attack dynamics.

In addition, I used Symantec's annual reports, specifically the "Internet Security Threat Report," to gather statistics and analysis on global trends regarding ransomware attacks. These reports are valuable since they offer a detailed view of the threat landscape and the ever-changing techniques used by cybercriminals.

The economic considerations related to cybercrime have been explored in depth in Moore and Clayton's work, "The Impact of the Economics of Cybercrime". This study sheds light on the economic motivations behind attackers to launch ransomware attacks, providing necessary context to understand the dynamics behind these crimes.

Information on emerging trends and threats in cyberspace was further integrated with Europol's "Internet Organised Crime Threat Assessment (IOCTA)" report, which revealed how ransomware has become a common weapon in the hands of criminal organisations. As well as Kaspersky's "Ransomware: A Global Threat Report", which provided up-to-date data and in-depth analysis of how these attacks are evolving over time.

Finally, I looked at the resources provided by the Federal Bureau of Investigation (FBI) regarding cybercrime, specifically their focus on ransomware. Official FBI information and concrete case studies enriched my understanding of defense strategies and preventive measures that victims can take.

In addition to these sources, I found Choi and Lee's article, "Understanding the Psychological Aspects of Cybercrime," enlightening, as it offered valuable insights into the psychological dynamics that affect both attackers and victims of ransomware attacks.

In summary, the wide range of sources consulted has made it possible to construct a text that is not only informative but also reflective, capable of addressing the many facets of ransomware, from the technical to the more human. I hope that this summary of the use of sources can offer a clear idea of the rigorous research work that has supported the writing of this book.

In a world where connection is power, the real strength lies in our ability to protect what is important to us or our companies, because digital security is not just an option, but a necessity.

Fabio Bessega